Play the Guitar
An Introduction

This book is divided into seven sections. If you progress through each one, and play a little everyday, you'll soon find yourself playing chords, experimenting with scales, and playing more easily with others.

1. **All the Basics** shows you how to tune your guitar, warm up and learn the basic hand positions – all essential for playing.

2. **First Chords** introduces simple chords and how to play them, before leading on to finger picking, intervals, triads and the difference between major and minor chords.

3. **Timing & Charts** explains timing and rhythm, with time signatures, chord charts and strumming patterns.

4. **Notes & Keys** will help you understand the basics of music notation, TAB, key signatures and how to work with major or minor keys.

5. **More Chords** extends the knowledge of the **First Chord** section: Sevenths, Sus chords, 5ths, Ninths, Extended and Altered, with chord substitution, inversions and Barre chords too.

6. **Scales & Keys** covers how to use major, pentatonic and minor scales, as well as dealing with transposition and pitch.

7. **More Skills** gives a few extra techniques: plectrum use, alternative tuning, arpeggios and octaves.

Don't forget to look at **flametreemusic.com** where chords and scales on your computer, mobile or tablet

D1609672

3

START
HERE

ALL THE
BASICS

FIRST
CHORDS

TIMING
& CHARTS

NOTES
& KEYS

MORE
CHORDS

SCALES
& PITCH

MORE
SKILLS

The Diagrams
A Quick Guide

The chord diagrams are designed for quick access and ease of use. Use the finger positions and fretboard to help you make the chord.

Each chord is provided with a *Chord Spelling* to help you check each note. This is a great way to learn the structure of the sounds you are making and will help with melodies and solo work.

Scale and arpeggio diagrams are shown in **player view**.

Top E
(1st string)

Bottom E
(6th string)

Fret
position

Fingerings
for each
note

Open
frets

Tabs help
give quick
access to
the sections

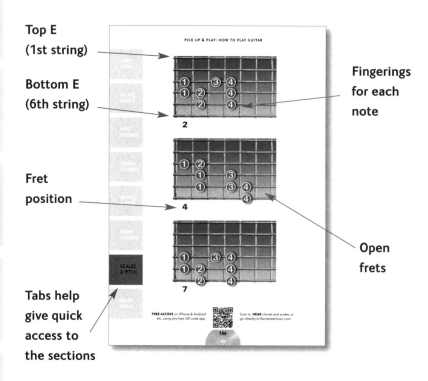

FREE ACCESS on iPhone & Android
etc, using any free QR code app

Scan to **HEAR** chords and scales, or
go directly to flametreemusic.com

Contents

Play the Guitar

An Introduction 3

The Diagrams

A Quick Guide 4

The Sound Links

Another Quick Guide 6

flametreemusic.com

The Website 176

Learn to Play.........8–175

All the Basics 8–21

First Chords 22–65

Timing & Charts 66–93

Notes & Keys 94–103

More Chords 104–29

Scales & Pitch 130–49

More Skills 150–75

Publisher/Creative Director: Nick Wells • Project, design and media integration: Jake Jackson • Website and software: David Neville with Stevens Dumpala and Steve Moulton • Editorial: Gillian Whitaker

First published 2016 by
FLAME TREE PUBLISHING
6 Melbray Mews, Fulham, London
SW6 3NS, United Kingdom
flametreepublishing.com

Music information site:
flametreemusic.com

16 17 18 19 20 21 22
2 3 4 5 6 7 8 9 10

© 2016 Flame Tree Publishing Ltd

All images and notation courtesy of Flame Tree Publishing, except the following: chord images, guitar and fretboard diagrams © 2016 Jake Jackson/Flame Tree Publishing Ltd; Creative Commons Attribution-Share Alike 2.0 Generic: 14 Przemek Jahr; 39 Bart Velo; 41 Man Alive!; 89 Johnyrc9; 135 Machocarioca; 140 Nick Soveiko; Creative Commons Attribution-Share Alike 4.0 Richard Szamelt; 138 Richard Szamelt; Shutterstock.com: 20 Iancu Cristian, 36 Funnyangel, 73 mffoto, 78 Brian A Jackson.

Android is a trademark of Google Inc. Logic Pro, iPhone and iPad are either registered trademarks or trademarks of Apple Computer Inc. in the United States and/or other countries. Cubase is a registered trademark or trademark of Steinberg Media Technologies GmbH, a wholly owned subsidiary of Yamaha Corporation, in the United States and/or other countries. Nokia's product names are either trademarks or registered trademarks of Nokia. Nokia is a registered trademark of Nokia

Corporation in the United States and/or other countries. Samsung and Galaxy S are both registered trademarks of Samsung Electronics America, Ltd. in the United States and/or other countries.

Every effort has been made to contact copyright holders. We apologize in advance for any omissions and would be pleased to insert the appropriate acknowledgement in subsequent editions of this publication.

Tony Skinner (original text) is the director of the Registry of Guitar Tutors – the world's foremost organization for guitar education. He is also the principal guitar examiner for London College of Music Exams and has compiled examination syllabi in electric, bass and classical guitar playing, as well as popular music theory, rock/pop band and popular music vocals. He has written and edited over 50 music-education books, and is the editor of Guitar Tutor magazine and a columnist for Total Guitar magazine.

Alan Brown (notation) is a former member of the Scottish National Orchestra. He now works as a freelance musician, with several leading UK orchestras, and as a consultant in music and IT. Alan has had several compositions published, developed a set of music theory CD-Roms, co-written a series of bass guitar examination handbooks and worked on over 100 further titles.

Jake Jackson (editor) is a writer and musician. He has created and contributed to over 25 practical music books, including Reading Music Made Easy. His music is available on iTunes, Amazon and Spotify amongst others.

No guitars were harmed during the making of this book. Guitars used include Fender 1977 Stratocaster, JJ special edition acoustic steel string, T.F. Morris acoustic steel string, Rickenbacker 360 semi-acoustic, Ramirez flamenco and Yamaha classical nylon string.

Printed in China

Title: Each chord is given a short and complete name, for example the short name C°7 is properly known as C Diminished 7th.

The Strings: The bass E appears on the left (6th string), the top E is on the right (1st string). The top E is the E above **middle C** on the piano.

E   A   D   G   B   E

Fingerings:
❶ is the index finger   ❷ is the middle finger
❸ is the ring finger   ❹ is the little finger

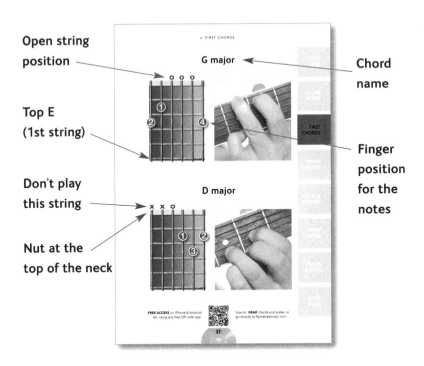

Open string position

Top E (1st string)

Don't play this string

Nut at the top of the neck

Chord name

Finger position for the notes

2. FIRST CHORDS

G major

D major

x x o

FREE ACCESS on iPhone & Android etc, using any free QR code app.   Scan to **HEAR** chords and scales, or go directly to flametreemusic.com

27

The Sound Links
Another Quick Guide

Requirements: a camera and internet ready smartphone (e.g. **iPhone**, any **Android** phone (e.g. **Samsung Galaxy**), **Nokia Lumia**, or **camera-enabled tablet** such as the **iPad Mini**). The best result is achieved using a WIFI connection.

1. Download any **free QR code reader**. An app store search will reveal a great many of these, so obviously it's best to go with the ones with the highest ratings and don't be afraid to try a few before you settle on the one that works best for you. Tapmedia's QR Reader app is good, or ATT Scanner (used below) or QR Media. Some of the free apps have ads, which can be annoying.

2. On your smartphone, open the app and **scan** the **QR code** at the base of any particular page.

FREE ACCESS on smartphones including iPhone & Android

Using any free QR code app, scan and **HEAR** the chord

78

3. The QR reader app will take you to a browser, then a specific scale will be displayed on flametreemusic.com.

4. Use the drop down menu to choose from **20 scales** or 12 **free chords** (50 with subscription) per key.

FREE ACCESS on iPhone & Android etc, using any free QR code app

Scan to **HEAR** chords and scales, or go directly to flametreemusic.com

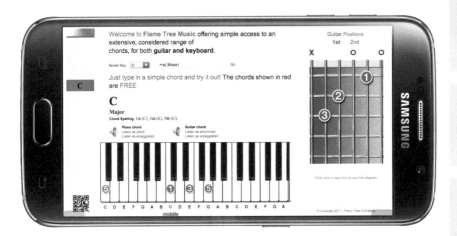

START
HERE

ALL THE
BASICS

FIRST
CHORDS

5. Using the usual pinch and zoom techniques, you can focus on four sound options.

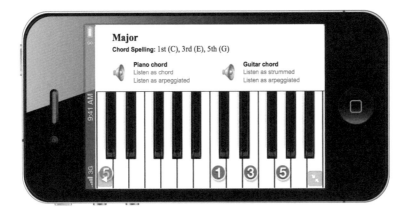

TIMING
& CHARTS

NOTES
& KEYS

MORE
CHORDS

6. Click the sounds! Both piano and guitar audio is provided. This is particularly helpful when you're playing with others.

The QR codes give you direct access to chords and scales. You can access a much wider range of chords if you register and subscribe.

FREE ACCESS on iPhone & Android etc, using any free QR code app

Scan to **HEAR** chords and scales, or go directly to flametreemusic.com

Tuning

Tuning is the first skill any guitarist has to master: no matter how well you play, it won't sound any good if the guitar is out of tune.

START
HERE

ALL THE
BASICS

FIRST
CHORDS

TIMING
& CHARTS

NOTES
& KEYS

MORE
CHORDS

SCALES
& PITCH

MORE
SKILLS

Instuner
(by EUMLab of Xanin Tech. GmbH)

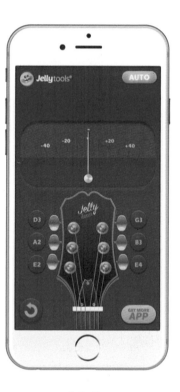

Jelly Tuner
(by Orphee Music)

ABOVE: Tuners come in many different shapes and sizes – mobile phone apps (for Apple iPhone, Android and Windows) are increasingly popular and easy to use.

FREE ACCESS on iPhone & Android
etc, using any free QR code app

Scan to **HEAR** chords and scales, or
go directly to flametreemusic.com

Pitch

A guitar can be tuned so that all the strings are 'in tune' with one another, and this can sound fine if you are playing alone or unaccompanied. However, if you intend to play with other musicians or along to a recording, then you'll need to make sure that your guitar is tuned to 'concert pitch'. Technically, that means that the note A, when played on the fifth fret of the first string (the A above middle C on a piano), is vibrating at 440 hertz (cycles per second). In practice, guitarists in a band will usually tune up to a keyboard or use an electronic tuner for reference. Acoustic guitarists sometime still use a tuning fork to find a 'true' pitch.

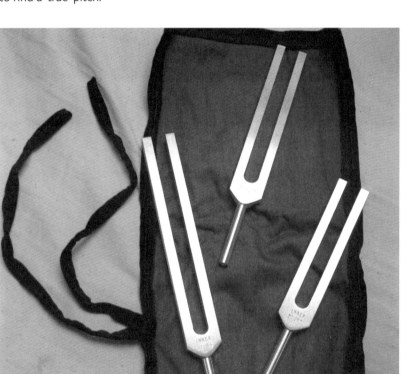

ABOVE: A tuning fork is normally used to find the 'true' pitch and is easy to carry in a small bag.

Tuning at the Fifth Fret

The open strings of the guitar, from the lowest note (thickest string) to the highest (thinnest string), should be tuned as follows.

finger pressed
down on fifth fret

finger pressed
down on fourth fret

Right hand will strike
second (B) and first
(E) string together

Tuning the top E string

Right hand will strike
third (G) and second (B)
string together

Tuning the top B string

Once you have tuned the low string to the pitch of E you can use this as the starting point from which to tune all the other strings.

FREE ACCESS on iPhone & Android etc, using any free QR code app

Scan to **HEAR** chords and scales, or go directly to flametreemusic.com

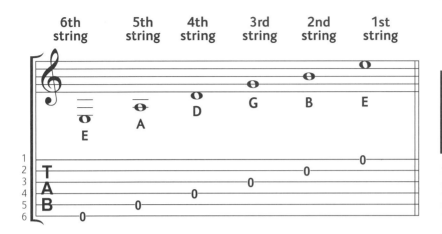

1. Begin by playing a note on the fifth fret of the low E string; this will produce the note A. You should then turn the fifth string machine head (tuning peg) until the pitch of this open string matches the fretted note on the lower string.

   If the open fifth string sounds higher than the fretted A note then you should rotate the machine head to slacken the string; if the open fifth string sounds too low then you should tighten the string.

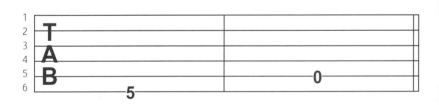

A on the 6th string   **Open A string**

ALL THE BASICS

2. Once you have tuned the A string, you can produce the note of D by picking a note at the fifth fret; this will provide you with the pitch you need to tune the open D string accurately.

You can then use the same method for tuning the open G string, i.e. by adjusting it to match the note played on the fifth fret of the D string.

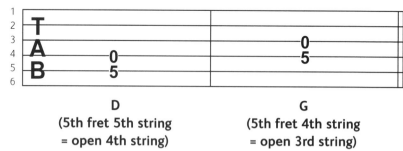

D	G
(5th fret 5th string = open 4th string)	**(5th fret 4th string = open 3rd string)**

3. The procedure changes slightly when you come to the B string. You need to tune this to the pitch of the note on the fourth fret of the G string.

Once the B string is in tune, fretting it at the fifth fret will produce the note E; you should adjust the open first string to match this pitch.

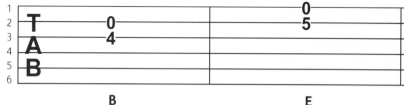

B	E
(4th fret 3rd string = open 2nd string)	**(5th fret 2nd string = open 1st string)**

FREE ACCESS on iPhone & Android etc, using any free QR code app

Scan to **HEAR** chords and scales, or go directly to flametreemusic.com

Once you've completed this process, listen closely to various chords at different positions on the neck and make any final tuning adjustments.

It's important to remember that a guitar is not a synthesizer, and characteristic imperfections in a guitar's components can affect its intonation (the accuracy of its pitch at all positions) as well as its tone. These characteristics are not necessarily bad things and can give a guitar a unique personality. They can also make it easier or harder to keep a guitar in tune.

ALL THE
BASICS

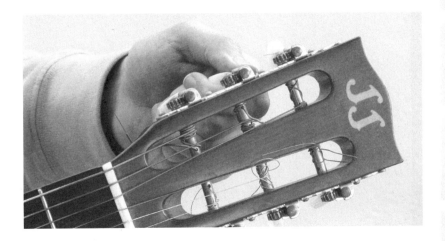

～TIPS～

Unless you are fitting new strings, you will not need to make large turns on the machine heads. If you tune your guitar regularly, then a few small tuning adjustments should be all it normally needs.

FREE ACCESS on iPhone & Android etc, using any free QR code app

Scan to **HEAR** chords and scales, or go directly to flametreemusic.com

Warming Up

Music may come from the head and heart, but your body gives the physical delivery – and that is why guitarists should be prepared. Just as with athletes, the best results will come when you have woken up the relevant muscles, rather than starting from cold.

Stretching your wrists, hands and fingers is a good starting point, and should precede any actual playing. Pressing palm to palm and bending each hand in turn to make a 90-degree angle – a little beyond, if possible – can be followed by bending back individual fingers. Repeat the process three or four times, then try pairs of fingers.

Exercise can help you avoid tendonitis, carpal tunnel syndrome and other repetitive stress injuries. But they can also help you play better and achieve greater speed.

ABOVE: The dazzling technique of Paco de Lucia required great care of his hands and fingers.

FREE ACCESS on iPhone & Android etc, using any free QR code app

Scan to **HEAR** chords and scales, or go directly to flametreemusic.com

ALL THE BASICS

STEP 1

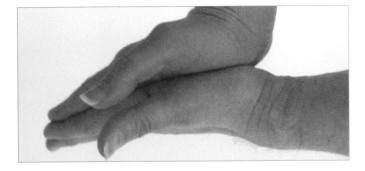

ALL THE
BASICS

STEP 2

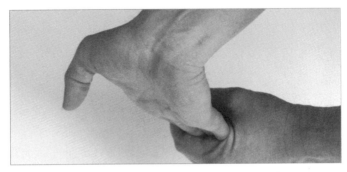

STEP 3

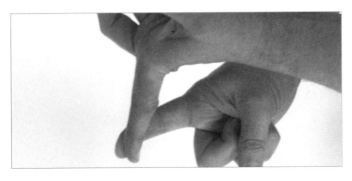

STEP 4

FREE ACCESS on iPhone & Android
etc, using any free QR code app

Scan to **HEAR** chords and scales, or
go directly to flametreemusic.com

Hand Positions

If you don't position your hands in the optimum way, learning to play guitar might prove to be an uphill struggle; playing with a good technique from the start, by positioning your hands correctly, will make learning new techniques relatively easy.

Fretting Hand

ALL THE
BASICS

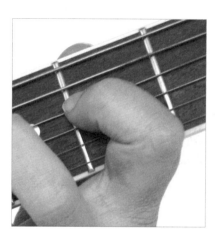

1. Regardless of whether you are playing chords or single notes, you should always press the fretting-hand fingers as close to the fretwire as possible. This technique minimizes the unpleasant 'fretbuzz' sounds that can otherwise occur. Pressing at the edge of the fret also greatly reduces the amount of pressure that is required, enabling you to play with a lighter and hence more fluent touch.

2. Try to keep all the fretting-hand fingers close to the fingerboard so that they are hovering just above the strings ready to jump into action. This minimizes the amount of movement required when moving from one chord or note to another. To do this, your

thumb should be placed at the centre of the back of the guitar neck, your fingers arching over the fretboard to descend more or less vertically on the strings.

3. Unless you are playing more than one note with the same finger, you should always use the tips of your fingers to fret notes; this will produce the sound more directly and cleanly than using the fleshier pads of the fingers.

ALL THE BASICS

ABOVE: The optimum position for your hand when you are fretting a note: fingers are close to the frets, which minimizes any fretbuzz.

FREE ACCESS on iPhone & Android etc, using any free QR code app

Scan to **HEAR** chords and scales, or go directly to flametreemusic.com

START HERE

ALL THE BASICS

FIRST CHORDS

TIMING & CHARTS

NOTES & KEYS

MORE CHORDS

SCALES & PITCH

MORE SKILLS

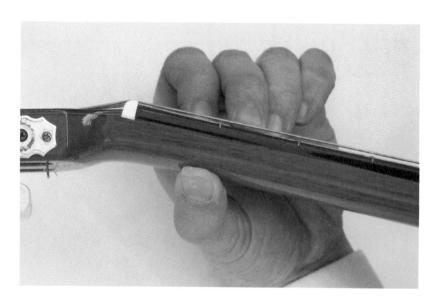

ABOVE: Correct hand position – your thumb should be placed at the centre of the back of the guitar neck, your fingers arching over the fretboard to descend more or less vertically on the strings.

FREE ACCESS on iPhone & Android etc, using any free QR code app

Scan to **HEAR** chords and scales, or go directly to flametreemusic.com

Picking Hand

1. If you're using a plectrum (pick), grip it between the index (first) finger and the thumb.

Position the plectrum so that its tip extends only just beyond the fingertip, by about $\frac{1}{10}$ in (25 mm). Whilst this measurement doesn't have to be exact, make sure that the amount of plectrum that extends beyond the index finger is not excessive: this would result in a lack of pick control, making the plectrum liable to flap around when striking the strings – reducing both fluency and accuracy.

If you find that when you try to pick a string you often miss it completely, the cause is most likely to be not enough plectrum extending beyond the fingertip.

START HERE

ALL THE BASICS

FIRST CHORDS

TIMING & CHARTS

NOTES & KEYS

MORE CHORDS

SCALES & PITCH

MORE SKILLS

START HERE

ALL THE BASICS

FIRST CHORDS

TIMING & CHARTS

NOTES & KEYS

MORE CHORDS

SCALES & PITCH

MORE SKILLS

2. Although you need to hold the plectrum with a small amount of pressure so that it doesn't get knocked out of your hand when you strike the strings, be very careful not to grip the plectrum too tightly.

Excessive gripping pressure can lead to muscular tension in the hand and arm, with a subsequent loss of flexibility and movement.

ABOVE: Avoid holding the plectrum at right angles to your index finger, otherwise your wrist may lock.

FREE ACCESS on iPhone & Android etc, using any free QR code app

Scan to **HEAR** chords and scales, or go directly to flametreemusic.com

3. The most efficient way to pick single notes is to alternate between downstrokes and upstrokes. Unless you want to achieve a particular staccato sound, this 'alternate picking' technique should be used for all melodies or lead-guitar playing. (For information on finger-picking, see pages 36–37.)

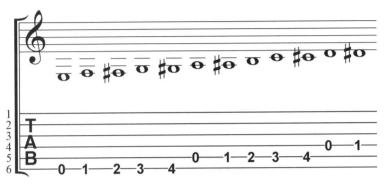

ABOVE: The E chromatic scale consists of a continual series of half steps, which means that every note in 'open position' is played. This makes the scale ideal for building technique as it uses all four fingers to fret notes. It should be played using alternate down and up plectrum strokes.

Scan to HEAR chords and scales, or go directly to flametreemusic.com

First Chords & Simple Sequences

Chords form the backbone of all music. As soon as you've mastered a few chord shapes you'll be well on the road to music-making. The really great thing about chords is that once you've learnt them they'll last you a lifetime: you'll still be using any chord you learn today 20 years from now.

Chord Symbols

There are two main types of chords that form the core of most popular music: 'major chords' and 'minor chords'.

G major

1. The chord symbol that tells you when to play a major chord is simply the letter name of the chord written as a capital. For example, the chord symbol for the G major chord is 'G' and the chord symbol for the D major chord is 'D'. Major chords have a bright, strong sound.

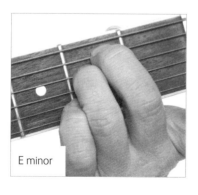

E minor

2. Minor chord symbols consist of the capital letter of the chord name followed by a lowercase 'm'. For example, the chord symbol for the E minor chord is 'Em' and the chord symbol for the A minor chord is 'Am'. Minor chords have a mellow, sombre sound.

FREE ACCESS on iPhone & Android etc, using any free QR code app

Scan to **HEAR** chords and scales, or go directly to flametreemusic.com

START HERE

ALL THE BASICS

FIRST CHORDS

TIMING & CHARTS

NOTES & KEYS

MORE CHORDS

SCALES & PITCH

MORE SKILLS

CHORD NAME	CHORD SYMBOL
C major	C
C minor	Cm
D major	D
D minor	Dm
E major	E
E minor	Em
F major	F
F minor	Fm
G major	G
G minor	Gm
A major	A
A minor	Am
B major	B
B minor	Bm

START HERE

ALL THE BASICS

FIRST CHORDS

TIMING & CHARTS

NOTES & KEYS

MORE CHORDS

SCALES & PITCH

MORE SKILLS

FREE ACCESS on iPhone & Android etc, using any free QR code app

Scan to **HEAR** chords and scales, or go directly to flametreemusic.com

START
HERE

ALL THE
BASICS

**FIRST
CHORDS**

TIMING
& CHARTS

NOTES &
ARPEGGIOS

MORE
CHORDS

SCALES
& PITCH

MORE
SKILLS

Fretboxes

Guitar chord fingerings are written in diagrams known as 'fretboxes'. These indicate the strings and frets that are used for the chord, and which fingers should be used for fretting the notes.

An O above a string line means this string should be played open (unfretted).

An X above a string line means this string should not be played.

The thick box at the top of the fretbox represents the nut of the guitar, and the remaining horizontal lines represent frets.

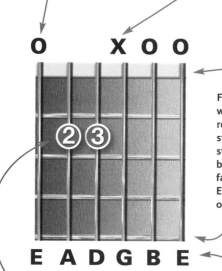

Fretboxes are written with vertical lines representing the strings: the low E string is represented by the line on the far left and the high E string by the line on the far right.

E A D G B E

The recommended fret-hand fingering is shown in simple numbered circles:

① = index finger
② = middle finger
③ = ring finger
④ = little finger

Notes of the open strings. The low E is on the left. (This is standard for right handed guitarists)

Starting Chords

Em

Am

G

D

Using the next few pages, begin with **E minor**, as this involves only two fretted notes and uses plenty of open strings.

Place your fingers on the strings, pressing lightly yet securely with the fingertips, and then **strum across all six strings**.

Once you're familiar with this chord, move your two fretting fingers from E minor on to the adjacent higher strings, and add the first finger on the first fret of the B string – this is **A minor**. Notice that the low E string should be omitted when you strum A minor.

Next try some **major chords**. If **G major** seems like too much of a stretch between the second and third fingers, allow your thumb to move down to the centre of the back of the guitar neck until the chord feels comfortable.

Notice that only the top four strings should be strummed when playing **D major**.

FREE ACCESS on iPhone & Android etc, using any free QR code app

Scan to **HEAR** chords and scales, or go directly to flametreemusic.com

E Minor

FIRST
CHORDS

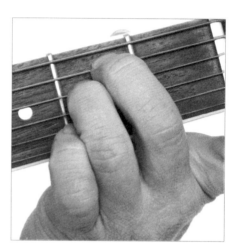

A Minor

FREE ACCESS on iPhone & Android
etc, using any free QR code app

Scan to **HEAR** chords and scales, or
go directly to flametreemusic.com

G Major

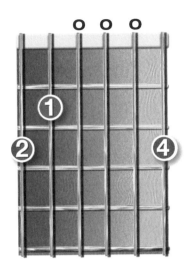

FIRST CHORDS

D Major

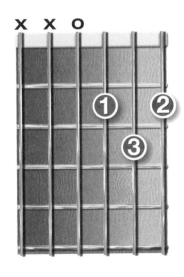

FREE ACCESS on iPhone & Android
etc, using any free QR code app

Scan to **HEAR** chords and scales, or
go directly to flametreemusic.com

Simple Chord Sequences

Many songs consist of a short chord sequence that is repeated throughout. Once you have learnt a couple of basic chord shapes you can start playing a chord sequence by changing from one chord to another. It's then only a short step before you can play the chords to a complete song.

Minor Chords

Begin by strumming downwards four times on an E minor chord, then without stopping change to A minor and play another four strums, keeping the same tempo. Without stopping or hesitating, move your fingers back to E minor and continue strumming so that the whole sequence begins again.

Notice the similarity of the **E minor** and **A minor** chord shapes: the second and third fingers are used at the second fret in both chords, the only difference being that they move from the A and D strings in E minor to the adjacent D and G strings in A minor. Try to keep this in mind when you change between these chords, so that you can minimize the amount of finger movement you make – this will make changing between the chords easier and quicker.

FREE ACCESS on iPhone & Android etc, using any free QR code app

Scan to **HEAR** chords and scales, or go directly to flametreemusic.com

Major Chords

Begin by playing four downstrums on a G major chord then, without stopping, move your fingers to D major and play another four strums. Repeat the sequence from the beginning by changing back to G major.

Try to keep an even tempo throughout and practise slowly until you are able to change between the chords without pausing or hesitating. Notice how the third finger stays at the third fret for both G and D major. Use this as a pivot point to lead the chord change.

Try to move all three fretting fingers as one shape when changing chord, rather than placing the fingers on one at a time; this will make the chord changes smoother.

FIRST CHORDS

$\frac{4}{4}$ ‖: G | D :‖

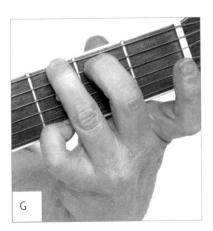

G

D

FREE ACCESS on iPhone & Android etc, using any free QR code app

Scan to **HEAR** chords and scales, or go directly to flametreemusic.com

Combining Chords

Once you feel fully familiar with the four chord shapes, try and combine them in this four-chord sequence, playing four downstrums for each chord.

$\frac{4}{4}$ **‖:** **G** | **Em** |

⊓ ⊓ ⊓ ⊓   ⊓ ⊓ ⊓ ⊓

Am | **D** **:‖**

⊓ ⊓ ⊓ ⊓   ⊓ ⊓ ⊓ ⊓

1. Look for any links between the different chord fingerings so that you can minimize the amount of finger movement you need to make.

2. Remember to place the fingers for each complete chord shape on the fretboard together, rather than finger by finger.

3. Practise very slowly so that you don't develop a habit of slowing down or stopping between chord changes.

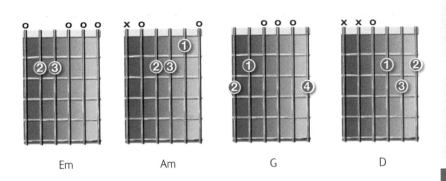

Em   Am   G   D

FIRST CHORDS

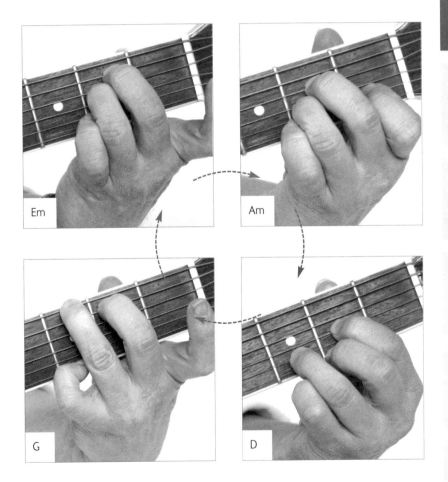

Em

Am

G

D

Scan to **HEAR** chords and scales, or go directly to flametreemusic.com

Strumming

Strumming chords forms the foundation of any guitar player's range of techniques. Strumming can be used to accompany your own or someone else's singing; it can also be used to provide a backing for lead-guitar playing. Being able to strum in a variety of styles will enable you to play rhythm guitar in a wide range of musical genres.

ABOVE: Strumming is an essential technique to master.

FREE ACCESS on iPhone & Android etc, using any free QR code app

Scan to **HEAR** chords and scales, or go directly to flametreemusic.com

Strum Technique

For the music to flow smoothly it's essential to develop a **relaxed strumming action**. It will aid the fluency of rhythm playing if the action comes from the wrist: a fluid and easy strumming action is best achieved this way, with the wrist loose and relaxed.

If the wrist is stiff and not allowed to move freely then excessive arm movement will occur, as the strumming action will be forced to come from the elbow instead. As this can never move as fluently as the wrist, there will be a loss of smoothness and rhythmic potential.

START HERE

ALL THE BASICS

FIRST CHORDS

TIMING & CHARTS

NOTES & ARPEGGIOS

SCALES & PITCH

MORE SKILLS

Strumming Exercises

START
HERE

ALL THE
BASICS

FIRST
CHORDS

TIMING
& CHARTS

NOTES &
ARPEGGIOS

MORE
CHORDS

SCALES
& PITCH

MORE
SKILLS

1. Begin by strumming an E minor chord using four downstrums per measure, and then experiment by inserting a quick upstrum between the second and third beats. The upstrum should be played by an upwards movement generated from the wrist, as though the strumming hand is almost effortlessly bouncing back into position ready for the next downstrum. Keep practising this technique until it feels natural, always making sure that the arm itself isn't moving up and down when you're strumming.

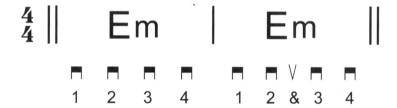

EXERCISE 1

2. Progress to adding two upstrums per bar: one between beats two and three, and one after the fourth beat. After the first two bars, try changing the chord to A minor and see if you can keep the strumming pattern going. If you can't change the chord quickly enough then start again from the beginning, playing at a much slower tempo.

3. To really get the strumming hand moving try adding an upstrum after every downstrum. Although this strumming style would be too busy for most songs, this exercise does provide practice in building a fluent strumming technique. Make sure that you have the plectrum positioned correctly, with its tip extending only just beyond the index fingertip, so that it does not drag on the strings as you strum.

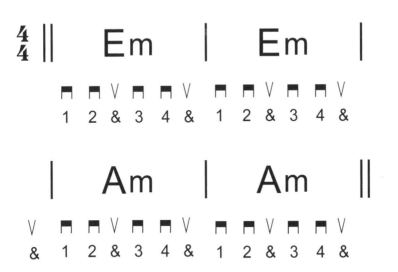

EXERCISE 2

EXERCISE 3

START
HERE

ALL THE
BASICS

FIRST
CHORDS

TIMING
& CHARTS

NOTES &
ARPEGGIOS

MORE
CHORDS

SCALES
& PITCH

MORE
SKILLS

Finger-picking

Finger-picking can provide a really interesting alternative to strumming. The technique is not just confined to classical or folk guitarists – many rock and pop players also use finger-picking as a method of bringing melodic interest to a chord progression and as a way of introducing musical subtleties to a song.

FREE ACCESS on iPhone & Android etc, using any free QR code app

Scan to **HEAR** chords and scales, or go directly to flametreemusic.com

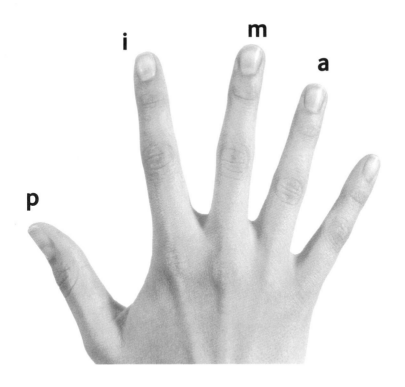

Fingering

In music notation, each picking finger is identified by a letter: '**p**' represents the thumb, '**i**' the index finger, '**m**' the middle finger and '**a**' the ring finger. (As it is much shorter than the others, the little finger is rarely used in finger-picking.)

⁓TIPS⁓

It's easier to finger-pick if you let your fingernails grow a little. Using nails to pick the strings will also give you a crisper, clearer and stronger sound.

Scan to **HEAR** chords and scales, or go directly to flametreemusic.com

START HERE

ALL THE BASICS

FIRST CHORDS

TIMING & CHARTS

NOTES & ARPEGGIOS

MORE CHORDS

SCALES & PITCH

MORE SKILLS

The thumb is mostly used for playing the bass strings (the lowest three strings), while the fingers are used for playing the treble strings.

There are many different ways of finger-picking, but one of the easiest is to use the 'a' finger for picking the first string, the 'm' finger for the second string and the 'i' finger for the third string.

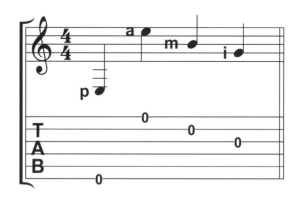

Picking Patterns

Many guitarists use a **repetitive finger-picking pattern** throughout a song to create a continuity of sound.

Picking patterns nearly always begin by playing the root note of the chord (i.e. the note that gives the letter name to the chord) on the bass string using the thumb.

For example, the **low E string** would be the first note of a pattern when finger-picking on a chord of **E minor**, and the **open A string** would be the first note when finger-picking on a chord of **A minor**.

Alternating Bass Pattern

If the picking pattern on a chord is repeated then sometimes a different bass is used the second time. This will normally be another note from the chord, usually the adjacent bass string. This technique can completely transform a simple chord progression, making it sound quite complex because of the moving bass line. This style of finger-picking is known as 'alternating bass'.

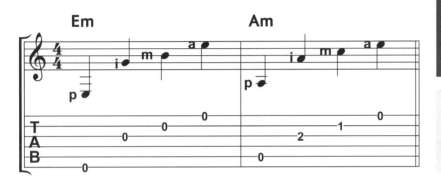

ABOVE: Two finger-picking guitarists will create a powerful, intricate sound.

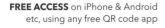

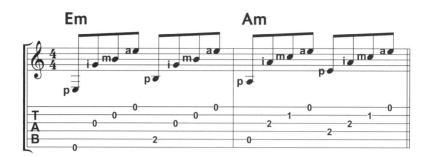

START HERE

ALL THE BASICS

FIRST CHORDS

TIMING & CHARTS

NOTES & ARPEGGIOS

MORE CHORDS

SCALES & PITCH

MORE SKILLS

In some musical styles, more complex picking patterns might be used on the treble strings. It is best to practise these types of patterns on one chord until the picking pattern feels totally comfortable. Once you are familiar with a pattern it's relatively easy to apply it to a chord progression. You just need to take care about which bass note to pick on each chord, ensuring you use the root note as your starting point.

ABOVE: Complex finger-picking requires a steady hand to aid speed.

FREE ACCESS on iPhone & Android
etc, using any free QR code app

Scan to **HEAR** chords and scales, or
go directly to flametreemusic.com

More Chords

The more chords you learn, the more songs you'll be able to play. Developing knowledge of even just the 10 most common chords will enable you to play thousands of songs (yes!), providing you practise them enough so that you can change fluently from chord to chord.

FIRST CHORDS

ABOVE: Ed Sheeran's mastery of chords contributes significantly to his success as a singer/songwriter.

FREE ACCESS on iPhone & Android etc, using any free QR code app

Scan to **HEAR** chords and scales, or go directly to flametreemusic.com

Main Chord Types

Although there are dozens of different chord types, all of these can be considered as just variations of the two core types of chords: major chords and minor chords. For example, if you come across a chord chart that includes Am7, playing a simple A minor chord will work almost as well.

However, developing a good knowledge of the most popular major and minor chords will provide a firm foundation for all future chord playing.

FIRST CHORDS

Major Chords

In addition to the G and D major chords that were covered on page 27, some other important major chords to start with are **A, C, E and F**.

Notice that all the strings can be strummed on the **E major** chord, whereas the sixth string should be omitted when the A or C chords are strummed.

The **F major chord** is different from the other chord fingerings in that the first finger needs to lie flat across both the first and second strings. You will find this easier if you ensure that your thumb is positioned quite low at the

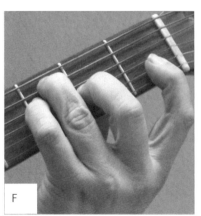
F

back of the guitar neck; this will help you keep your first finger flat while the second and third fingers press with the fingertips.

Make sure that you only strum the top four strings when playing the F major chord.

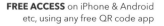

A Major

C Major

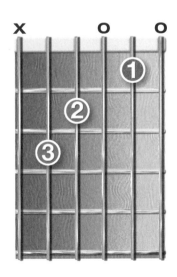

Scan to **HEAR** chords and scales, or
go directly to flametreemusic.com

FIRST
CHORDS

E Major

F Major

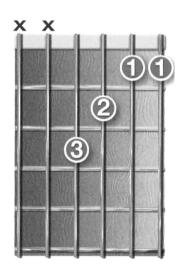

Shown here using the top four strings only.

FREE ACCESS on iPhone & Android etc, using any free QR code app

Scan to **HEAR** chords and scales, or go directly to flametreemusic.com

Minor Chords

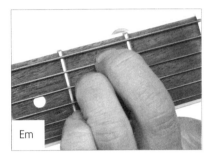

Em

In addition to the Em and Am chords that were covered on page 26, the other most important minor chords to learn at first are **Dm** and **F#m**. Both Dm and F#m are four-string chords (i.e. the fifth and sixth strings should be omitted when playing these chords).

The F#m chord is a development of the technique that you gained when learning to play the F major chord, but this time the first finger needs to fret **all** the **top three strings**.

Am

If you find this tricky, you might like to try resting the second finger on top of the first finger; this will add extra weight and strength to help the first finger hold down all three strings. Positioning the fretting finger as close as possible to the fretwire will reduce the amount of finger pressure required.

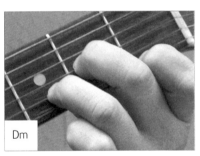

Dm

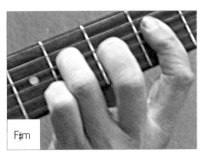

F#m

Second supporting finger

FIRST CHORDS

FIRST
CHORDS

Dm

F#m

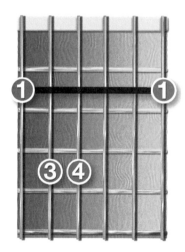

Shown here using the top four strings only.

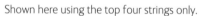

FREE ACCESS on iPhone & Android
etc, using any free QR code app

Scan to **HEAR** chords and scales, or
go directly to flametreemusic.com

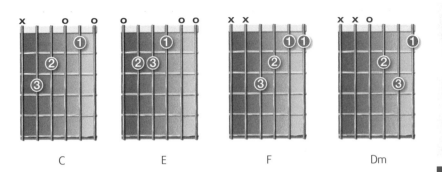

C E F Dm

Try this chord combination

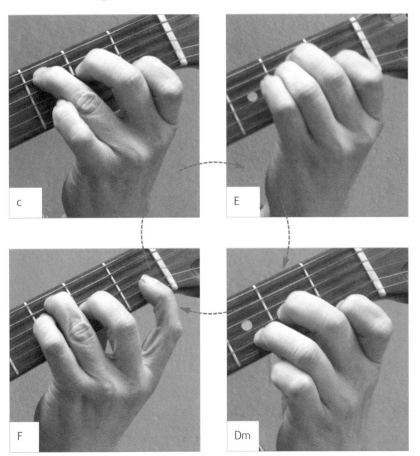

C

E

F

Dm

FREE ACCESS on iPhone & Android
etc, using any free QR code app

Scan to **HEAR** chords and scales, or
go directly to flametreemusic.com

Intervals

Intervals are the spaces between notes from the major scale, or other scales. Chords are constructed by combining various intervals. The name of a chord is often based upon the largest interval contained within that chord.

Major Second

A major second is the interval from the first to the second note of the major scale (e.g. in the key of C, from C to D).

Major Second (a short interval)

Major Second to Major Ninth

If you play the major second note an octave higher it forms a major ninth interval. This interval is included in all major ninth, minor ninth and dominant ninth chords.

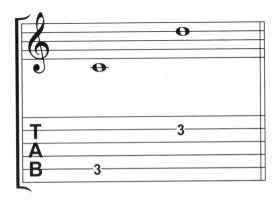

Major Ninth (a long interval)

Major Third

A major third is the interval from the first to the third note of the major scale (e.g. in the key of C, from C to E). This interval is important in that it defines the tonality of a chord; a chord that is constructed with a major third interval from its root note will always be a type of major chord.

START HERE

ALL THE BASICS

FIRST CHORDS

TIMING & CHARTS

NOTES & ARPEGGIOS

MORE CHORDS

SCALES & MODES

MORE SKILLS

START
HERE

ALL THE
BASICS

FIRST
CHORDS

TIMING
& CHARTS

NOTES &
ARPEGGIOS

MORE
CHORDS

SCALES
& PITCH

MORE
SKILLS

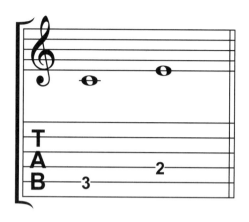

Major Third

If you lower the major third interval by a half step it becomes a minor third. Just as the major third interval determines that a chord has a major tonality, the minor third interval determines that a chord is minor.

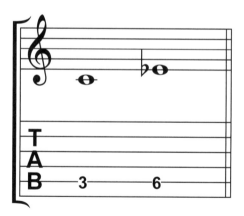

Minor Third

FREE ACCESS on iPhone & Android etc, using any free QR code app

Scan to **HEAR** chords and scales, or go directly to flametreemusic.com

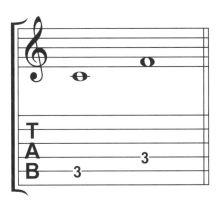

Perfect Fourth

Perfect Fourth

A perfect fourth is the interval from the first to the fourth note of the major scale (e.g. in the key of C, from C to F).

Perfect Fifth

A perfect fifth is the interval from the first to the fifth note of the major scale (e.g. in the key of C, from C to G). The perfect fifth occurs in nearly all chords, apart from diminished or augmented chords.

If you lower the perfect fifth interval by a half step it becomes a diminished (flattened) fifth. This interval occurs in diminished chords and any chords labelled with a flattened fifth note. If you raise the perfect fifth interval by a half step it becomes an augmented (sharpened) fifth. This interval occurs in augmented chords and any chords labelled with a sharpened fifth note.

FREE ACCESS on iPhone & Android etc, using any free QR code app

Scan to **HEAR** chords and scales, or go directly to flametreemusic.com

51

START
HERE

ALL THE
BASICS

FIRST
CHORDS

TIMING
& CHARTS

NOTES &
ARPEGGIOS

MORE
CHORDS

SCALES
& PITCH

MORE
SKILLS

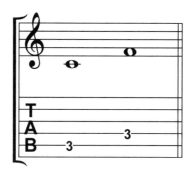

Perfect Fourth

Diminished Fifth

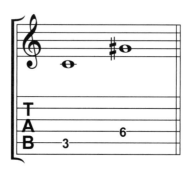

Augmented Fifth

FREE ACCESS on iPhone & Android
etc, using any free QR code app

Scan to **HEAR** chords and scales, or
go directly to flametreemusic.com

Major Sixth

A major sixth is the interval from the first to the sixth note of the major scale (e.g. in the key of C, from C to A). The major sixth occurs in both major and minor sixth chords. If you add an octave to a major sixth it becomes a major 13th interval. This interval is used in all 13th chords.

Major Sixth

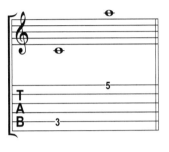

Major 13th

Major Seventh

A major seventh is the interval from the first to the seventh note of the major scale (e.g. in the key of C, from C to B). The major seventh interval occurs in major seventh chords. If you lower the major seventh interval by a half step it becomes a minor seventh. This interval occurs in both minor seventh and dominant seventh chords.

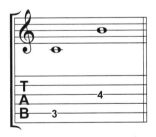

Major Seventh

Minor Seventh

FREE ACCESS on iPhone & Android etc, using any free QR code app

Scan to **HEAR** chords and scales, or go directly to flametreemusic.com

START HERE

ALL THE BASICS

FIRST CHORDS

TIMING & CHARTS

NOTES & ARPEGGIOS

MORE CHORDS

SCALES & PITCH

MORE SKILLS

Major Triads

Chords that contain three different notes are known as 'triads'. All standard major chords are triads. All other chords, no matter how elaborate, can be considered simply as variations or extensions of these triads. Therefore, learning all the major triads will provide a firm foundation for learning any other chords.

The **first**, **third** and **fifth** notes of the major scale make up a major triad. For example, the C major triad is formed by taking the first, third and fifth notes of the C major scale.

C major triad

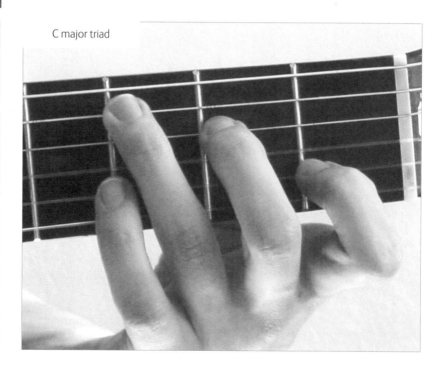

ABOVE: The standard C major shape on a guitar includes two C notes, one as the root, the other on the second string, an octave above.

START HERE

ALL THE BASICS

FIRST CHORDS

TIMING & CHARTS

NOTES & ARPEGGIOS

MORE CHORDS

SCALES & PITCH

MORE SKILLS

You can work out which notes are in any major triad by selecting the first, third and fifth notes from the major scale with the same starting note as the chord. This would give the following:

C Major Scale

1	2	3	4	5	6	7	8
C	D	E	F	G	A	B	C

C Major Triad

C   E   G

C	G	D	A
Major Triad	Major Triad	Major Triad	Major Triad
C E G	G B D	D F♯ A	A C♯ E
Notes in Triad	Notes in Triad	Notes in Triad	Notes in Triad

E	B	F♯	F
Major Triad	Major Triad	Major Triad	Major Triad
E G♯ B	B D♯ F♯	F♯ A♯ C♯	F A C
Notes in Triad	Notes in Triad	Notes in Triad	Notes in Triad

B♭	E♭	A♭	D♭
Major Triad	Major Triad	Major Triad	Major Triad
B♭ D F	E♭ G B♭	A♭ C E♭	D♭ F A♭
Notes in Triad	Notes in Triad	Notes in Triad	Notes in Triad

START HERE

ALL THE BASICS

FIRST CHORDS

TIMING & CHARTS

NOTES & ARPEGGIOS

MORE CHORDS

SCALES & PITCH

MORE SKILLS

FREE ACCESS on iPhone & Android etc, using any free QR code app

Scan to **HEAR** chords and scales, or go directly to flametreemusic.com

Although major triads only contain three different notes, strumming three-string chords could result in quite a thin sound, so quite often major chords are played with some of the notes doubled so that five or six strings can be strummed.

For example, in the open position **G major chord** below:

- the **G note** is played **three** times (on the sixth, third and first strings)

- the **B note** is played **twice** (on the fifth and second strings)

- the **D note** is played **once**

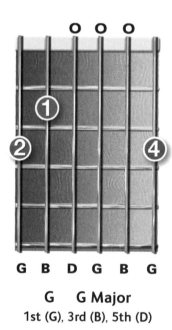

G   B   D   G   B   G

G   G Major
1st (G), 3rd (B), 5th (D)

Now that you know the notes contained in each major triad you can devise as many different fingerings for each chord as you wish. To help you get started, there follows one fretbox example for **each major triad**.

FREE ACCESS on iPhone & Android etc, using any free QR code app

Scan to **HEAR** chords and scales, or go directly to flametreemusic.com

X O O

A E A C♯ E

A   A Major
1st (A), 3rd (C♯), 5th (E)

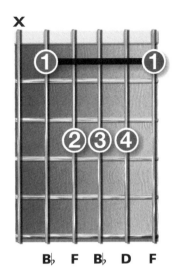

X O O

B♭ F B♭ D F

B♭/A♯   B♭ Major
1st (B♭), 3rd (D), 5th (F)

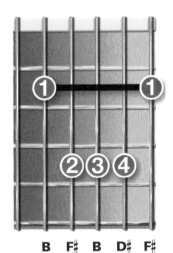

B F♯ B D♯ F♯

B   B Major
1st (B), 3rd (D♯), 5th (F♯)

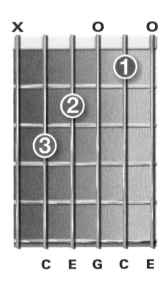

X O O

C E G C E

C   C Major
1st (C), 3rd (E), 5th (G)

Scan to **HEAR** chords and scales, or go directly to flametreemusic.com

FIRST CHORDS

FIRST
CHORDS

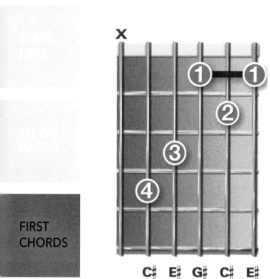

C♯ E♯ G♯ C♯ E♯

C♯/D♭   C♯ Major
1st (C♯), 3rd (E♯), 5th (G♯)

D A D F♯

D   D Major
1st (D), 3rd (F♯), 5th (A)

3

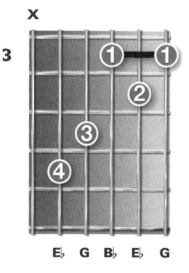

E♭ G B♭ E♭ G

E♭/D♯   E♭ Major
1st (E♭), 3rd (G), 5th (B♭)

E B E G♯ B E

E   E Major
1st (E), 3rd (G♯), 5th (B)

FREE ACCESS on iPhone & Android
etc, using any free QR code app

Scan to **HEAR** chords and scales, or
go directly to flametreemusic.com

F   F Major
1st (F), 3rd (A), 5th (C)

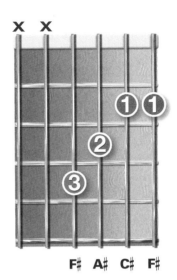

F♯/G♭   F♯ Major
1st (F♯), 3rd (A♯), 5th (C♯)

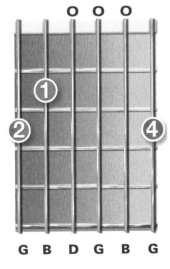

G   G Major
1st (G), 3rd (B), 5th (D)

A♭/G♯   A♭ Major
1st (A♭), 3rd (C), 5th (E♭)

FREE ACCESS on iPhone & Android
etc, using any free QR code app

Scan to **HEAR** chords and scales, or
go directly to flametreemusic.com

Minor Triads

Minor triads have a more mellow, mournful sound than major triads but, just like major triads, they also contain only three different notes. All other minor chords are built on the foundation of these minor triads, so learning at least the most common minor triads is essential for any rhythm-guitar player.

FIRST
CHORDS

- Minor triads contain the **first**, **flattened third** and **fifth notes** of the major scale. (The flattened third note can be found one fret lower than the major third note.)

- For example, the C minor triad contains the notes C, E♭, and G. Taking the first, third and fifth notes from the natural minor scale will give the same results.

- You can work out which notes are in any minor triad by selecting the first, third and fifth notes from the natural minor scale with the same starting note as the chord.

C minor

Remember that although triads consist of only three different notes, you can repeat one or more of the notes when playing them as chords on the guitar.

C Natural Minor Scale

1	2	3	4	5	6	7	8
C	D	E♭	F	G	A♭	B♭	C

C Minor Triad

C   E♭   G

Am	**Em**	**Bm**	**F♯m**
Minor Triad	Minor Triad	Minor Triad	Minor Triad
A C E	E G B	B D F♯	F♯ A C♯
Notes in Triad	Notes in Triad	Notes in Triad	Notes in Triad
C♯	**G♯m**	**D♯m**	**Dm**
Minor Triad	Minor Triad	Minor Triad	Minor Triad
C♯ E G♯	G♯ B D♯	D♯ F♯ A♯	D F A
Notes in Triad	Notes in Triad	Notes in Triad	Notes in Triad
Gm	**Cm**	**Fm**	**B♭m**
Minor Triad	Minor Triad	Minor Triad	Minor Triad
G B♭ D	C E♭ G	F A♭ C	B♭ D♭ F
Notes in Triad	Notes in Triad	Notes in Triad	Notes in Triad

FREE ACCESS on iPhone & Android etc, using any free QR code app

Scan to **HEAR** chords and scales, or go directly to flametreemusic.com

FIRST
CHORDS

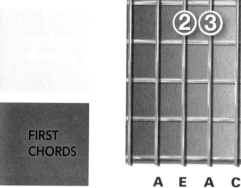

X O   O

A E A C E

Am   A Minor
1st (A), ♭3rd (C), 5th (E)

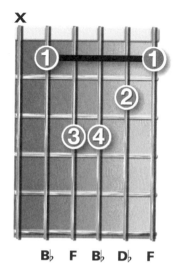

X

B♭ F B♭ D♭ F

B♭m/A♯m   B♭ Minor
1st (B♭), ♭3rd (D♭), 5th (F)

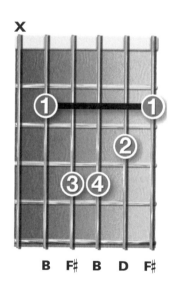

X

B F♯ B D F♯

Bm   B Minor
1st (B), ♭3rd (D), 5th (F♯)

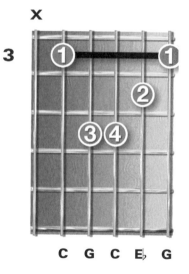

X

3

C G C E♭ G

Cm   C Minor
1st (C), ♭3rd (E♭), 5th (G)

FREE ACCESS on iPhone & Android
etc, using any free QR code app

Scan to **HEAR** chords and scales, or
go directly to flametreemusic.com

FIRST
CHORDS

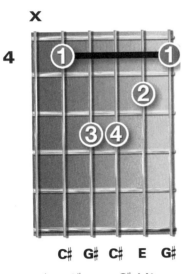

X

4

C♯ G♯ C♯ E G♯

D♭m/C♯m   C♯ Minor
1st (C♯), ♭3rd (E), 5th (G♯)

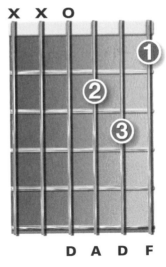

X X O

D A D F

Dm   D Minor
1st (D), ♭3rd (F), 5th (A)

X X

E♭ B♭ E♭ G♭

E♭m/D♯m   E♭ Minor
1st (E♭), ♭3rd (G♭), 5th (B♭)

O O O O

E B E G B E

Em   E Minor
1st (E), ♭3rd (G), 5th (B)

FREE ACCESS on iPhone & Android
etc, using any free QR code app

Scan to **HEAR** chords and scales, or
go directly to flametreemusic.com

FIRST
CHORDS

F A♭ C A♭ C F

Fm   F Minor
1st (F), ♭3rd (A♭), 5th (C)

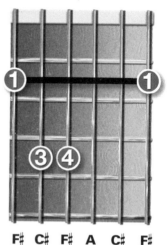

F♯ C♯ F♯ A C♯ F♯

F♯m/G♭m   F♯ Minor
1st (F♯), ♭3rd (A), 5th (C♯)

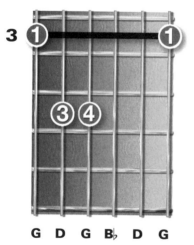

G D G B♭ D G

Gm   G Minor
1st (G), ♭3rd (B♭), 5th (D)

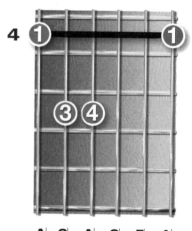

A♭ C♭ A♭ C♭ E♭ A♭

A♭m/G♯m   A♭ Minor
1st (A♭), ♭3rd (C♭), 5th (E♭)

FREE ACCESS on iPhone & Android
etc, using any free QR code app

Scan to **HEAR** chords and scales, or
go directly to flametreemusic.com

Other Triads

As well as major and minor triads, there are other triads:

- **diminished**
- **augmented**
  (see **C Augmented** chord below)
- **suspended**
  (see **C sus4** chord below)

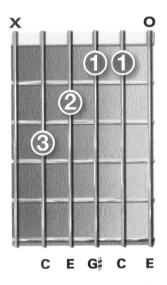

C E G♯ C E

C+ C Augmented
1st (C), 3rd (E), ♯5th (G♯)

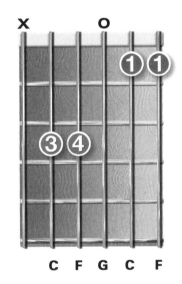

C F G C F

Csus4 C Suspended 4th
1st (C), 4th (F), 5th (G)

Timing

The most important skill any rhythm-guitar player needs is the ability to maintain an even tempo and keep in time with other band members. It's essential that your rhythm playing sits in the same groove as the other members of the rhythm section.

Developing Timing Skills

Some people have a natural sense of rhythm and timing that just needs nurturing, while others have to concentrate on developing a secure sense of timing.

A simple test to evaluate your sense of timing is to try and clap along to a recording by one of your favourite bands.

- While listening to the recording, focus your attention on the drums and try to clap a regular beat that matches the main rhythmic pulses within the song.

- Listen carefully to your clapping and see if you can stay in time throughout the whole song – **stamina** is an important aspect of rhythm playing.

Before you try to play through a song make sure that you have mastered any technical challenges, such as awkward chord changes, in advance. Otherwise, the temptation will be to slow down when approaching the difficult bits and perhaps speed up on the easy bits.

TIMING
& CHARTS

Try to avoid developing poor timing habits from the start by always **choosing a slow practice tempo** at which you can master the whole song – difficult bits and all!

Once you can play the song without any mistakes or hesitations, it's relatively easy to gradually increase the tempo each time you practise.

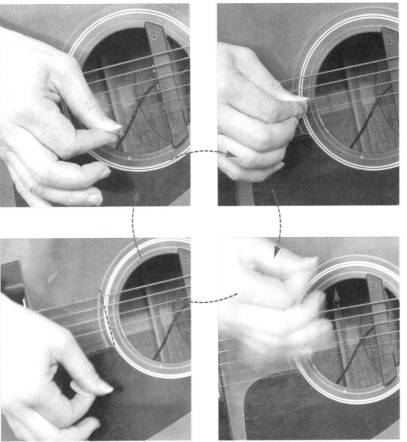

TIMING
& CHARTS

ABOVE: Keeping strict time is critical, even when varying the technique. Here, two quick alternating strums are followed by a full upstroke across all strings, then a solid downstroke.

Timing Aids

Ideally you should always try to practise your rhythm playing with a device that keeps regular time. The simplest method is to practise with a **metronome**. This is a small mechanical or electronic device that sounds a click on each beat. You can set it to click in increments from a very slow to a super-fast tempo. It's always best to practise anything new at a slow tempo, increasing the metronome setting by a couple of notches each time you've successfully played it the whole way through.

A drum machine can be used instead of a metronome. The advantage of the drum machine is that you can set it to play back interesting drum patterns to help inspire your strumming style. You can programme the machine, or use preset patterns, so that it emulates different musical genres.

TIMING
& CHARTS

ABOVE and RIGHT: Metronomes are now available in a range of traditional and mobile forms.

iMaschine iPhone app
(Native Instruments GmbH)

FREE ACCESS on iPhone & Android etc, using any free QR code app

Scan to **HEAR** chords and scales, or go directly to flametreemusic.com

Playing along to records is also a good method of developing a secure sense of timing: the band on the recording won't wait around if you lose time or hesitate over a chord change. Because there will be a longer space between beats, playing along with songs at a slow tempo emphasizes any timing inconsistencies – so don't forget to practise a few ballads alongside the thrash metal!

Electronic drum machines provide flexible and complex metronome functions.

⁓ TIPS ⁓

Record yourself playing along to a CD or a drum machine. Listen carefully to hear if your playing is exactly in time.

FREE ACCESS on iPhone & Android etc, using any free QR code app

Scan to **HEAR** chords and scales, or go directly to flametreemusic.com

Time Signatures

The time signature is the most important element in setting the musical feel and mood of a piece of music. It provides the framework for the rhythmic structure of a song and plays a large part in establishing the character of the music.

Recognizing Time Signatures

The symbol indicating the time signature is always written at the start of the music or chord chart. The time signature is normally written as two numbers, one above the other. The top number represents the number of beats per measure (bar), while the bottom number refers to the type of beats.

The most common time signature used in all styles of popular music is $\frac{4}{4}$ time. This indicates that there are four beats in a measure, and that these are quarter notes (crotchets). Sometimes the $\frac{4}{4}$ symbol is replaced with **C**, meaning 'common time'.

Note that the time signature only tells you the number and type of 'beats' that will occur in a measure; this is not the same as the number of 'notes' you can play in the measure. For example, a measure of music in $\frac{4}{4}$ time will last for the equivalent duration of four quarter beats, but in this space you might play fewer longer-lasting notes or more shorter notes. In fact, you can play any combination of long, medium or short notes providing the duration per measure is equivalent to four quarter-note beats. (See pages 73–77 for more information on understanding rhythm notation.)

Other Commonly Used Time Signatures

$\frac{2}{4}$ has two quarter-note beats per measure. This time signature tends to give a march-like feel to the music. Sometimes $\frac{2}{4}$ symbol is replaced with a ¢ symbol, meaning 'cut time'.

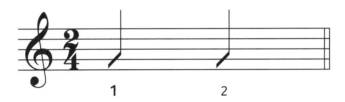

$\frac{3}{4}$ this has three quarter-note beats per measure. This time signature gives a waltz-like character to the music and is often used in country and folk ballads.

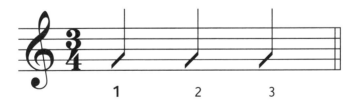

$\frac{2}{2}$ has two half-note beats per measure. This is equivalent in length to $\frac{4}{4}$ time, but with two long beats per measure instead of four quarter-note beats.

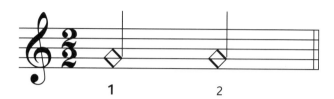

$\frac{6}{8}$ has six eighth-note beats per measure. However, these are normally played as two groups of three.

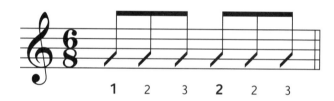

Establishing the Time Signature

If you were just to play a long series of chords all of equal strength it would be hard for the listener to recognize any rhythmic structure in the music – in other words, they wouldn't be able to 'feel the groove'. So normally the first beat of each measure is slightly accented, as this helps the sense of rhythm in a piece of music. In $\frac{6}{8}$ time an accent is normally played on the first of each group of three notes. (If you're playing in a band it might be the drums or other instruments that emphasize these accents.)

Scan to **HEAR** chords and scales, or go directly to flametreemusic.com

Rhythm Notation

Understanding how rhythms are written down will help you play through notated chord charts. The ability to notate your own rhythms is useful for passing the information to other players and as a memory aid. Even if you intend to rely mainly on tablature, a knowledge of rhythm notation will help you get the most out of the many song transcriptions that provide the full notation with the tab.

Note Values

Rhythm notation consists of pitchless notes and rests. The type of note used tells you how many beats a chord lasts; the type of rest used tells you how many beats a silence lasts. The diagram overleaf shows the names of the most common types of notes, their symbols and how many of each type of note can occur in a single measure in $\frac{4}{4}$ time.

TIMING & CHARTS

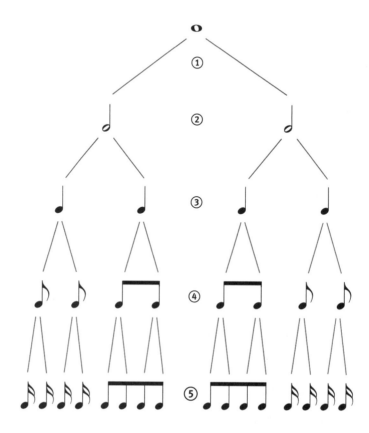

Whole note	①	Semibreve
Half notes	②	Minims
Quarter notes	③	Crotchets
Eighth notes	④	Quavers
Sixteenth notes	⑤	Semiquavers

ABOVE: The terminology used widely in North America (and increasingly amongst pop, rock and jazz musicians in the UK and elsewhere) is different from that traditionally used by classical musicians in many parts of the world. In the key above the modern names are shown on the left and the traditional names are shown on the right.

TIMING & CHARTS

Rests

The table below shows the names of the most common types of rests, their symbols, their note equivalents, and the duration of each type of rest in $\frac{4}{4}$ time.

Name	Rest Symbol	Note Equivalent	Duration in $\frac{4}{4}$ Time
semibreve rest (whole rest)	▬	𝅝	4 beats
minim rest (half rest)	▬	𝅗𝅥	2 beats
crotchet rest (quarter rest)	𝄽	𝅘𝅥	1 beat
quaver rest (eighth rest)	𝄾	𝅘𝅥𝅮	1/2 beat
semiquaver rest (16th rest)	𝄿	𝅘𝅥𝅯	1/4 beat

Scan to **HEAR** chords and scales, or go directly to flametreemusic.com

Dotted Notes

A dot after a note or rest means that the note or rest lasts for half as long again. This chart shows the values of dotted notes and dotted rests in $\frac{4}{4}$ time.

Name	Note	Rest	Duration in $\frac{4}{4}$ Time
dotted minim (half rest)	𝅗𝅥.	▬.	3 beats
dotted crotchet (quarter rest)	♩.	𝄽.	1 ½ beats
dotted quaver (eighth rest)	♪.	𝄾.	1 ¾ beat

Ties

A curved line known as a 'tie' is used to join together two notes of the same pitch in order to increase the duration of the note.

ABOVE: In this example, the first chord would be allowed to sustain for the equivalent of five eighth notes. It is not possible to use a dot after the initial chord as this would have increased the duration of the note to the equivalent of six eighth notes.

TIMING & CHARTS

Another common instance where ties are used is across bar lines as a method of sustaining a note beyond the end of a measure.

ABOVE: In this example, a tie is used so that the chord at the end of measure one can sustain into measure two.

Triplets

A triplet sign indicates where three notes should be played in the space of two notes of the same value.

TIMING & CHARTS

Chord Charts

Simple chord charts are the most commonly-used way of notating the chord structure of a song or progression. If you audition for a pop or rock band, the music you'll be asked to play will most likely be presented as a simple chord chart.

Reading Chord Charts

A chord chart normally has the time signature written at the very beginning. If there is no time signature then it's usually safe to assume that the music is in $\frac{4}{4}$ time.

TIMING & CHARTS

Each measure is separated by a vertical line, with two vertical lines indicating the end of the piece. Chord symbols are used to show which chords should be played.

Split Measures

When more than one chord appears in a single measure it can be assumed that the measure is to be evenly divided between the chords that appear within it.

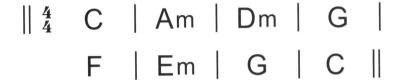

In a song in $\frac{3}{4}$ time, if three chords all appear in the same measure then you can assume that the measure is to be divided equally – with one beat per chord.

In many chord charts, in order to make the intention clear and avoid confusion, any division within a measure is shown by either a dot or a diagonal line after each chord: each dot or diagonal line indicates another beat.

Interpreting Chord Charts

In standard chord charts, while the duration of each chord is clearly shown, the rhythm style that should be played is left to the discretion of the performer. In theory this means that you could interpret the chart in any way you wish in terms of the number of strums per beat, however you should make sure that your rhythm playing relates to the musical style and mood of the song.

‖ 4/4 C ╱ Am ╱ |Dm ╱ G ╱ |
F ╱ Em ╱ |G ╱ C ╱ ‖

ABOVE: Each chord lasts for two beats: one beat indicated by the chord symbol and an additional beat indicated by the diagonal line.

TIMING & CHARTS

‖ 4/4 C Em ╱ ╱ | F G ╱ ╱ |
Am Em ╱ ╱ |G C ╱ ╱ ‖

ABOVE: In this example, the first chord in each measure lasts for just one beat and the second chord lasts for three beats.

‖ 4/4 C . . Dm |Em . . F |
Dm . . G |F . . C ‖

ABOVE: In this example, instead of diagonal lines, dots are used to show the rhythmic divisions within each measure. The first chord in each measure lasts for three beats and the second chord lasts for one beat.

FREE ACCESS on iPhone & Android etc, using any free QR code app

Scan to **HEAR** chords and scales, or go directly to flametreemusic.com

Following Chord Charts

If every bar of a whole song were written out in a chord chart it would take up several pages and become cumbersome to read. Instead chord charts are normally abbreviated by using a number of 'repeat symbols'. In order to follow a chord chart accurately it is essential to understand what each repeat symbol means.

Repeat Symbols

This symbol is used when one bar is to be repeated exactly.

✕. This symbol is used when more than one bar is to be repeated.

✕. The number of bars to be repeated is written above the symbol.

ABOVE: In this example, the chord chart above will be played as the chart below.

TIMING & CHARTS

81

START
HERE

ALL THE
BASICS

FIRST
CHORDS

TIMING
& CHARTS

NOTES &
ARPEGGIOS

MORE
CHORDS

SCALES
& PITCH

MORE
SKILLS

Section Repeats

The symbol of a double bar-line followed by two dots indicates the start of a section, and the symbol of two dots followed by a double bar-line indicates the end of the section to be repeated. If there are no dots at the start of the section, then repeat the music from the beginning of the piece. If the section is to be repeated more than once, the number of times it is to be played is written above the last repeat symbol.

If two sections of music are identical, except for the last measure or measures, repeat dots are used in conjunction with first-time and second-time ending directions:

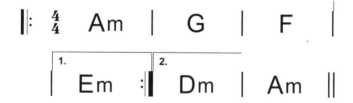

ABOVE: In this example too, the chord chart above will be played as the chart below.

$$\| \; {}^4_4 \; Am \mid G \mid F \mid Em \mid Am \mid$$
$$G \mid F \mid Dm \mid Am \|$$

FREE ACCESS on iPhone & Android etc, using any free QR code app

Scan to **HEAR** chords and scales, or go directly to flametreemusic.com

As well as repeat dots there are several other commonly used repeat signs:

- **D.C.** (an abbreviation of ***Da Capo***) means play 'from the beginning'. For example, if the entire piece of music is to be repeated, D.C. can be written at the end to instruct you to play it again from the beginning.

- **D.S.** (an abbreviation of ***Dal Segno***) means play 'from the sign': 𝄋. For example, if the verse and chorus of a song are to be repeated, but not the introduction, **D.S.** can be written at the end of the music with the **D.S.** sign written at the start of the verse. This instructs the performer to start again from the sign.

- **Coda** is the musical term for the end section of a piece of music. The start of the coda is marked by the sign: ⨁

- **Fine** is the musical term for the end of a piece of music.

Some of the above repeat signs might be combined in a chord chart.

ABOVE: In this example, after eight measures repeat from the beginning and then end after measure four where the sign 'Fine' appears.

FREE ACCESS on iPhone & Android etc, using any free QR code app Scan to **HEAR** chords and scales, or go directly to flametreemusic.com

START
HERE

ALL THE
BASICS

FIRST
CHORDS

TIMING
& CHARTS

NOTES &
ARPEGGIOS

MORE
CHORDS

SCALES
& PITCH

MORE
SKILLS

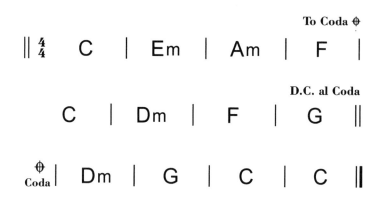

ABOVE: In this example, after eight measures repeat from the beginning and then after measure four jump to the coda section.

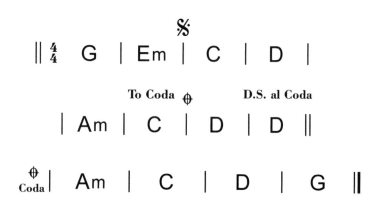

ABOVE: In this example, after eight measures repeat from the start of measure three to the end of measure six, then jump to the coda section.

FREE ACCESS on iPhone & Android etc, using any free QR code app

Scan to **HEAR** chords and scales, or go directly to flametreemusic.com

Rhythm Charts

While standard chord charts are commonly used by pop and rock bands, more detailed and complex charts known as 'rhythm charts' are often presented to guitarists involved in recording sessions and those who play in theatre and function band settings. Learning to read rhythm charts will help expand your employability as a guitarist.

Chart Styles

Some rhythm charts can be quite elaborate and may include a fully notated rhythm part, as well as detailed instructions about dynamics and tempo.

Others may contain notated rhythms only at the beginning, in order to establish the feel of the song, with further rhythm notation only being used where specific rhythmic accents or features occur.

The type of rhythm charts you come across will depend on the context and the transcriber's personal preferences.

Dynamic Markings

Symbols are often used in rhythm charts to indicate changes in volume – e.g. when you should play softly and when you should strum strongly.

- The symbols do not refer to any precise decibel volume level, instead their main function is to highlight changes in overall volume.

- The most common dynamic markings are shown overleaf. Accents, where certain individual beats are played stronger than others, are marked by this accent sign: >.

- The letters 'sfz' (*sforzando*) may be also used to indicate an accent.

START
HERE

ALL THE
BASICS

RHYTHM
& NOTES

TIMING
& CHARTS

NOTES &
ARPEGGIOS

MORE
CHORDS

SCALES
& PITCH

MORE
SKILLS

Symbol	Name	Meaning
pp	*pianissimo*	very soft
p	*piano*	soft
mp	*mezzo-piano*	medium soft
mf	*mezzo-forte*	medium loud
f	*forte*	loud
ff	*fortissimo*	very loud
<	*crescendo*	getting louder
>	*diminuendo*	getting softer

Italian Term	Meaning	Approx speed
Largo	very slow	40–60 b.p.m.
Adagio	slow	50–75 b.p.m.
Andante	walking pace	75–100 b.p.m.
Moderato	moderate tempo	100–120 b.p.m.
Allegro	fast	120–160 b.p.m.
Presto	very quick	160–200 b.p.m.

START HERE

ALL THE BASICS

FIRST CHORDS

TIMING & CHARTS

NOTES & ARPEGGIOS

MORE CHORDS

SCALES & PITCH

MORE SKILLS

FREE ACCESS on iPhone & Android etc, using any free QR code app

Scan to **HEAR** chords and scales, or go directly to flametreemusic.com

Tempo

Most rhythm charts will contain an indication of the speed at which the music should be played; this is usually written at the start of the music. The tempo indication may appear in either traditional Italian musical terms or their English equivalents.

Alternatively, a metronome marking may be shown to indicate the exact number of beats per minute (b.p.m.). The most common tempos are shown in the table below. Some music may contain changes in tempo. These are usually indicated through the use of Italian terms.

The most widely used are:

Italian Term	Meaning
Accel.	(an abbreviation of *accelerando*) means play gradually faster.
A tempo	indicates that you should resume the normal tempo after a deviation.
Meno mosso	(less movement) means that you should slow down at once.
Rall.	(an abbreviation of *rallentando*) means play gradually slower.
Rit.	(an abbreviation of *ritenuto*) means to hold back the tempo.

Playing Rhythm Charts

Below you'll see a sample rhythm chart, incorporating some of the terms and symbols described above. Refer to pages 74–77 if you need to be reminded of the note values.

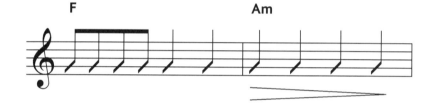

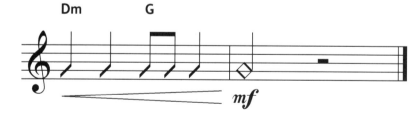

FREE ACCESS on iPhone & Android etc, using any free QR code app

Scan to **HEAR** chords and scales, or go directly to flametreemusic.com

Strumming Patterns

Building up a repertoire of useful strumming patterns is a good way of developing your rhythm-guitar playing. Once you've mastered the core patterns used in rock and pop you can easily expand these by adding variations.

Strum Technique

Playing with a loose wrist action is an essential ingredient of developing a good strumming technique. Keeping the wrist tight and strumming by using the whole forearm will severely restrict the potential speed and fluency of your rhythm playing – so make sure that the strumming action comes from your wrist. It's a good idea to practise in front of a mirror, or record a video of yourself playing guitar, so that you can see if you're using the right technique.

TIMING
& CHARTS

ABOVE: Rodrigo y Gabriela are an incredible Mexican duo who mix flamenco and heavy metal rhythms in their strumming, flamenco and solo techniques.

FREE ACCESS on iPhone & Android etc, using any free QR code app

Scan to **HEAR** chords and scales, or go directly to flametreemusic.com

89

Chord Technique

Be careful not to over-grip with the fretting-hand thumb on the back of the neck as this will cause muscle fatigue and tend to limit freedom of the thumb to move. The fretting-hand thumb must move freely when changing chords. If the thumb remains static this restricts the optimum positioning of the fingers for the next chord, which may result in unnecessary stretching

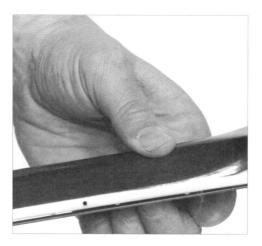

and the involuntary dampening of certain strings (as the fingers are not positioned upright on their tips). Be aware that for the fingers to move freely the wrist, elbow and shoulder must be flexible and relaxed. Make sure your standing or sitting position doesn't restrict the movement of your hands and arms.

ABOVE: Make sure you hold the thumb in opposition to the fingers, behind the neck, but don't press too hard.

Strum Patterns

On pages 91–93 you'll find several examples of popular strumming patterns. It's a good idea to start by playing all the progressions using just four downstrums per measure – this way you'll become familiar with the chord changes before tackling the strum patterns. In nearly all styles of music, there is no need to strum all the strings on every beat – feel free to add variety, particularly by omitting some bass strings on upstrokes and some treble strings on downstrokes.

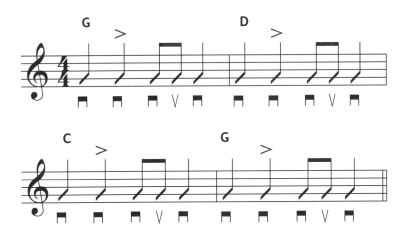

ABOVE: The second beat of the measure is accented to create dynamic variety. An upstroke is used after the third beat of the measure.

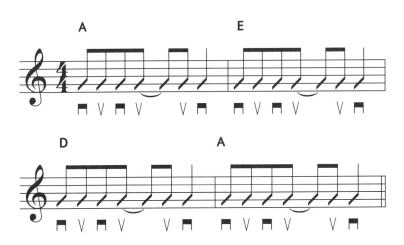

ABOVE: This pattern uses a mixture of down- and upstrokes, but notice how the fourth strum and the last strum are held longer than the others. This variety creates an effective rhythm.

FREE ACCESS on iPhone & Android etc, using any free QR code app

Scan to **HEAR** chords and scales, or go directly to flametreemusic.com

TIMING
& CHARTS

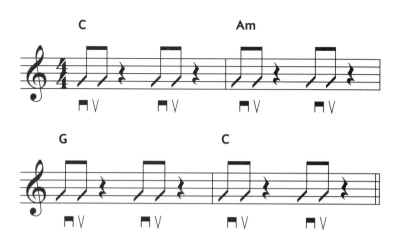

ABOVE: A simple down-up strum pattern, but the use of rests creates a very distinctive rhythmic effect.

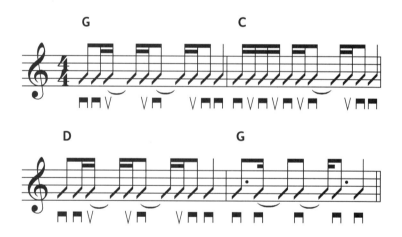

ABOVE: This 'Bo Diddley' type pattern is a good example of how to use rhythmic variations: notice that measures 1 and 3 are the same, while measures 2 and 4 are each variations on the first measure.

FREE ACCESS on iPhone & Android etc, using any free QR code app

Scan to **HEAR** chords and scales, or go directly to flametreemusic.com

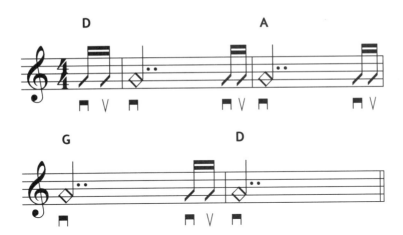

ABOVE: This typical rock strumming pattern is essentially just one strum per measure. What makes it distinctive is the rapid down-up 'pre-strum' before the main beat. These 'pre-strums' do not need to be played across all the strings, and open strings can be used on the second of them to help get to the main chord quickly.

TIMING & CHARTS

FREE ACCESS on iPhone & Android etc, using any free QR code app

Scan to **HEAR** chords and scales, or go directly to flametreemusic.com

Basics of Notation

There are three ways in which scales, licks and solos are written down: traditional notation, tablature and fretboxes. While you don't need to be a great sight-reader to play lead guitar, having a good understanding of each of the notation systems will help you learn lead guitar relatively easily.

Tablature

Tablature (TAB) uses six lines to represent the six strings of the guitar, with the top line representing the high E string and the bottom line representing the low E string.

Numbers are written on the lines to indicate which fret to play at. A zero indicates that the string is played open. TAB is great for notating scales or chords and, although it doesn't usually include any rhythm notation, its simplicity makes it ideal for learning music that you have heard before.

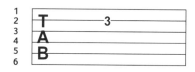

LEFT: This means play at the third fret on the second string.

Music Notation

Traditional music notation is written on a staff of five lines. Each line, and each space between the lines, represents a different note. For guitar music, a treble clef is written at the start of each line of music. Temporary extra lines (ledger lines) are used for any notes that are either too high or too low to fit on the staff.

**NOTES
& KEYS**

FREE ACCESS on iPhone & Android etc, using any free QR code app

Scan to **HEAR** chords and scales, or go directly to flametreemusic.com

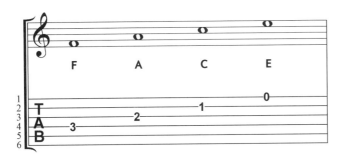

ABOVE: Notes on the spaces in the treble clef.

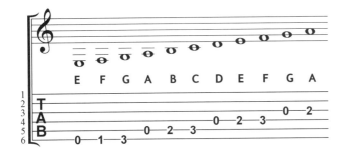

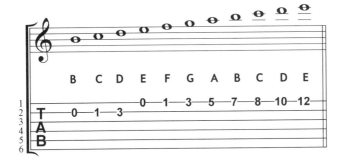

ABOVE: Using ledger lines, this diagram shows the notes from the open low E string to the E at the 12th fret on the first string.

Scan to **HEAR** chords and scales, or go directly to flametreemusic.com

NOTES & KEYS

A sharp sign (♯) is written in front of a note, on the same line or space, to raise its pitch by a half step (semitone) i.e. equivalent to one fret higher.

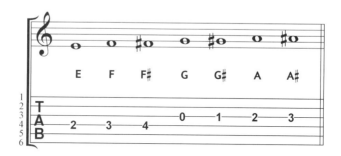

NOTES & KEYS

A flat sign (♭) is written in front of a note, on the same line or space, to lower its pitch by a half step (semitone). Any sharps or flats affect all the notes of the same pitch within the bar. A natural sign (♮) on the same line or space is used to cancel the previous sharp or flat.

Key Signatures

The key of a piece of music determines the main notes that will be included in it. In music notation a key signature is written at the beginning of every line of music to indicate the key. Key signatures make music easier to read because any sharps or flats in the key need only be written at the start of each line and will then apply to all those notes throughout the piece, rather than needing to write a sharp or flat sign every time such a note occurs.

G major
E minor

Each major key has a unique key signature, consisting of a collection of sharps or flats written in a set order; these sharps and flats match those that occur in the major scale for that key. The key of C major is unusual in that no sharps or flats occur in the keyscale, and therefore the key signature is blank.

E major
C♯ minor

Minor keys share key signatures with their relative major keys (i.e. **major keys** that have a keynote **three half steps higher** than that of the **minor key**).

NOTES & KEYS

| G major | D major | A major |
| E minor | B minor | F# minor |

| E major | B major | F# major |
| C# minor | G# minor | D# minor |

ABOVE: Sharp key signatures.

| F major | B♭ major | E♭ major |
| D minor | D minor | C minor |

| A♭ major | D♭ major | G♭ major |
| F minor | D minor | E♭ minor |

ABOVE: Flat key signatures.

Scan to **HEAR** chords and scales, or go directly to flametreemusic.com

Keys

The 'key' of a song refers to its overall tonality, and dictates which scale will be used as the basis of the melody and which chords fit naturally into the arrangement. Understanding which chords go together in a key will help you work out the chord structure of songs, and will provide a framework to begin writing your own songs.

Major Keys

In each major key, three major chords occur – as shown below:

Key	Major Chords in the Key		
C major	C	F	G
G major	G	C	D
D major	D	G	A
A major	A	D	E

Scan to **HEAR** chords and scales, or go directly to flametreemusic.com

START
HERE

ALL THE
BASICS

FIRST
CHORDS

TIMING
& CHARTS

NOTES
& KEYS

MORE
CHORDS

SCALES
& PITCH

MORE
SKILLS

A song or chord progression will normally begin with the **tonic (keynote)** chord. This is the **chord** that has the **same name as the key**. For example, in the key of C major, C is the tonic (keynote) chord.

Minor chords also occur in major keys. Some of the most commonly used minor chords in the keys of C, G, D and A major are shown below.

Key	Minor Chords in the Key		
C major	Dm	Em	Am
G major	Am	Bm	Em
D major	Em	F#m	Bm
A major	Bm	Dm	F#m

Although there are no fixed rules about which chords can be combined when you are composing a song or chord progression, if you select chords from the same key they will always fit together well.

Here's an example of a chord progression using 6 chords in the key of C major.

$$\| \quad C \quad | \quad Dm \quad | \quad Em \quad | \quad F \quad |$$
$$Am \quad | \quad G \quad | \quad F \quad | \quad C \quad \|$$

ABOVE: Chord progression in the key of C major.

FREE ACCESS on iPhone & Android etc, using any free QR code app

Scan to **HEAR** chords and scales, or go directly to flametreemusic.com

Minor Keys

In each minor key, **three minor chords** are closely related, and most commonly occur in popular songs.

For example, in the key of **A minor** the chords of **Am**, **Dm** and **Em** are the most important.

Three major chords also occur **in each minor key**. For example, in the key of **A minor**, **C**, **F** and **G major** chords occur.

As all these chords are within the same key they can be combined in any order (after starting with the tonic/keynote chord) to make a pleasant-sounding chord sequence.

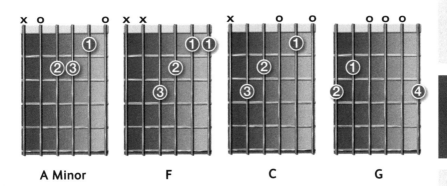

| A Minor | F | C | G |

An example is shown on the following page, but you can experiment with rearranging the chords in a different order and then playing them through to hear the musical result.

On the two pages that follow are a few chord progressions demonstrating some of the **most common chord sequences** used in a few of the most popular major and minor keys.

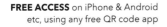

‖ Am │ F │ G │ C │
Am │ Dm │ Em │ Am ‖

ABOVE: Chord progression in the key of A minor.

‖ G │ D │ C │ G │
Em │ Am │ D │ G ‖

ABOVE: Chord progression in the key of G major.

‖ D │ Em │ F♯m │ Em │
G │ A │ G │ D ‖

ABOVE: Chord progression in the key of D major.

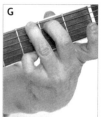

FREE ACCESS on iPhone & Android
etc, using any free QR code app

Scan to **HEAR** chords and scales, or
go directly to flametreemusic.com

‖ C | G | Am | Am |
F | Em | Dm | C ‖

ABOVE: Chord progression in the key of C major.

‖ A | E | F♯m | E |
D | E | A | A ‖

ABOVE: Chord progression in the key of A major.

‖ Em | D | C | D |
Am | G | D | Em ‖

ABOVE: Chord progression in the key of E minor.

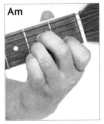

START HERE

ALL THE BASICS

RHYTHM & NOTES

TIMING & CHARTS

NOTES & KEYS

MORE CHORDS

SCALES & PITCH

MORE SKILLS

Chord Construction

When you've studied the basic major and minor chords on the previous pages, you'll find that there's good news: all other chords can be viewed as variations or extensions of the basic chords. To convert the basic triads into other chords, all that's normally required is to add to the triad a note from the major scale.

Sixth Chords

To work out how to play any major sixth chord you just play through the major scale until you reach the sixth note in the scale. Find the name of this note and then add this note to the basic major triad – thereby converting it into a major sixth chord.

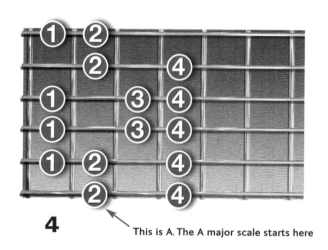

4

This is A. The A major scale starts here

It's helpful see the **A major scale** before looking at the opposite page.
The scale pattern is: A B C♯ D E F♯ G♯ A

For example, to play **A major 6** (A6) you should add F♯ (the **sixth note** of the **A major scale**) to the A major chord. (You will find an F♯ note on the second fret of the first string.)

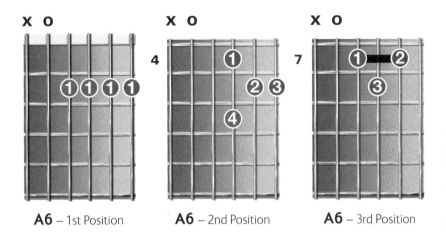

A6 – 1st Position   **A6** – 2nd Position   **A6** – 3rd Position

Minor sixth chords are formed in the same way, by adding the sixth note of the major scale to the minor triad. Notice that you **always** use the **major scale – even if the chord is minor!**

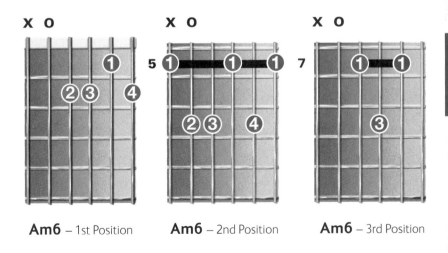

Am6 – 1st Position   **Am6** – 2nd Position   **Am6** – 3rd Position

MORE CHORDS

Seventh Chords

There are three main types of seventh chord:

- major seventh (maj7)
- dominant seventh (7)
- minor seventh (m7)

Only the **major seventh chord** uses the **seventh note** of the **major scale**; the other two types use the **flattened seventh** note of the scale.

The **major seventh chord** is formed by taking the **basic major chord** and adding the seventh note of the major scale to it.

For example, Amaj7 contains the notes A C# E G#.

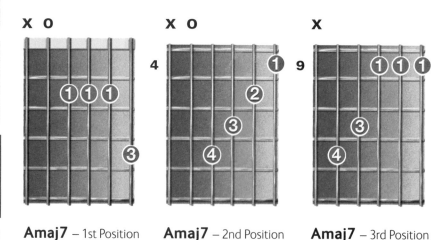

Amaj7 – 1st Position   **Amaj7** – 2nd Position   **Amaj7** – 3rd Position

MORE CHORDS

The **dominant seventh chord** is formed by taking the basic major chord and **adding the flattened seventh note** of the major scale to it. For example, A7 contains the notes A C♯ E G.

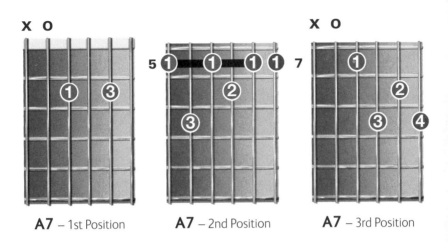

A7 – 1st Position   **A7** – 2nd Position   **A7** – 3rd Position

The **minor seventh chord** is formed by taking the **basic minor chord** and **adding** the **flattened seventh note** of the major scale to it. For example, Am7 contains the notes A C E G.

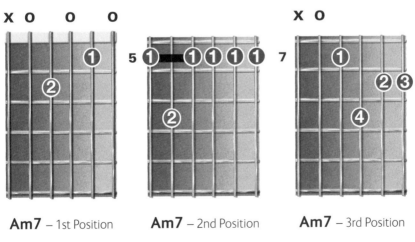

Am7 – 1st Position   **Am7** – 2nd Position   **Am7** – 3rd Position

MORE
CHORDS

FREE ACCESS on iPhone & Android etc, using any free QR code app

Scan to **HEAR** chords and scales, or go directly to flametreemusic.com

Sus Chords

Some chords are formed by **replacing** a note, rather than adding one.

Sus chords are a good example of this, as the chord's **third** is **replaced** by the **fourth** note of the major scale in sus4 chords, and by the **second** note of the scale in sus2 chords.

For example, Asus2 contains the notes A B E, and Asus4 contains the notes A D E.

Asus2

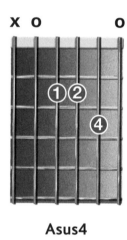

Asus4

ᕱᑑ TIPS ᑑᕱ

When adding notes to chords, it's normally best if you can find the note in a higher register, such as on the first string, before looking for it on the lower strings. Sometimes you might need to take a finger off a string to allow the new note to sound.

Scan to **HEAR** chords and scales, or go directly to flametreemusic.com

Fifth Chords

Fifth chords are unusual in that they do not include a major or minor third. They consist only of the root note and the fifth.

For example, A5 contains the notes A and E. In rock music, a prime example of the **fifth chord** is the '**power chord**', in which the root note and the fifth above it are played on the sixth and fifth, or fifth and fourth strings. With the right combination of electric guitar, amp and effects, this powerful sound characterizes hard rock and heavy metal.

A5

MORE
CHORDS

⌇TIPS⌇

Look carefully at the root note here. The A5 chord is easily confused with Asus2 except that the bass note E is sounded on the A5.

Extended & Altered Chords

Using extended chords, containing five or six notes, helps to create a rich sound and to extend your chordal vocabulary. Altered chords provide an ideal method of creating a sense of tension and adding harmonic dissonance to a chord progression.

Extended Chords

Just as seventh chords are built by adding an extra note to a basic triad, extended chords are built by adding one or more extra notes to a seventh chord. The most common types of extended chords are ninths, 11ths and 13ths. Each can be played in either a major, minor or dominant form. The example below is built on A major (A, C♯, E)

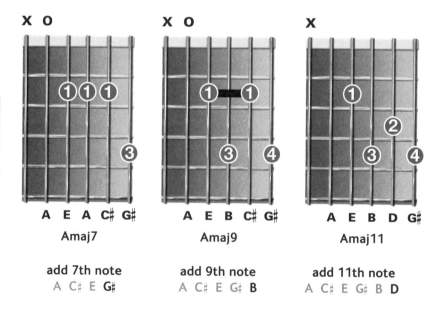

A E A C♯ G♯	A E B C♯ G♯	A E B D G♯
Amaj7	Amaj9	Amaj11
add 7th note	add 9th note	add 11th note
A C♯ E G♯	A C♯ E G♯ B	A C♯ E G♯ B D

FREE ACCESS on iPhone & Android etc, using any free QR code app

Scan to **HEAR** chords and scales, or go directly to flametreemusic.com

MORE CHORDS

Ninth Chords

Major ninth chords are extensions of major seventh chords. They are formed by **adding** the **ninth** note of the major scale (with the same starting note) to a major seventh chord. The interval spelling is **1 3 5 7 9**.

For example, Cmaj9 contains the notes C E G B (the notes of Cmaj7) **plus** the note of **D** (the ninth note of the C major scale). Major ninth chords have a delicate sound that makes them highly suitable for use in ballads.

C   E   B   D   E

Cmaj9

MORE
CHORDS

～TIPS～

Sometimes not all of the notes in a triad are played in a guitar chord (the G is missing in the Cmaj9 above), when the extended or altered notes are required.

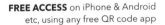

Dominant ninth chords are formed by adding the ninth note of the major scale to a dominant seventh chord.

C9

For example, C9 contains the notes C E G B♭ (the notes of C7) plus D (the ninth note of the C major scale). The interval spelling is 1 3 5 ♭7 9. Dominant ninth chords have a rich, bluesy sound.

MORE
CHORDS

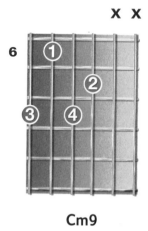

Cm9

Minor ninth chords are extensions of minor seventh chords, formed by adding the ninth note of the major scale.

For example, Cm9 contains C E♭ G B♭ (the notes of Cm7) plus D (the ninth note of the C major scale).

The interval spelling is 1 ♭3 5 ♭7 9. Minor ninth chords have a suave, mellow sound and are often used in soul and funk music.

Eleventh Chords

There are three main types of 11th chord as shown here.

You'll notice that each incorporates some form of ninth chord, plus the 11th note of the major scale. In practice, the ninth note is normally omitted when playing 11th chords on the guitar.

Chord Spelling for 11ths	
11 (Dominant 11th):	1 3 5 ♭7 9 11
m11 (Minor 11th):	1 ♭3 5 ♭7 9 11
maj11 (Major 11th):	1 3 5 7 9 11

MORE CHORDS

START
HERE

ALL THE
BASICS

FIRST
CHORDS

TIMING
& CHARTS

NOTES
& KEYS

MORE
CHORDS

SCALES
& PITCH

MORE
SKILLS

C11

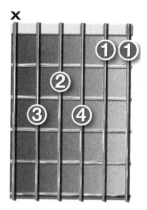
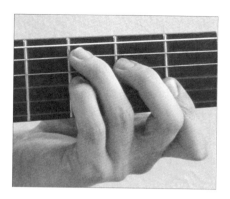

Cm11

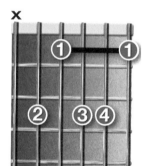

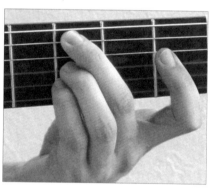

Cmaj11

4

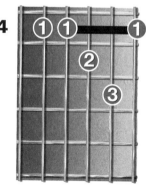

FREE ACCESS on iPhone & Android
etc, using any free QR code app

Scan to **HEAR** chords and scales, or
go directly to flametreemusic.com

Thirteenth Chords

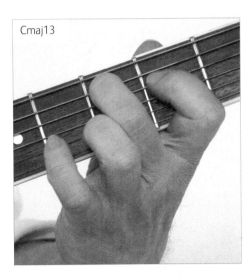

Cmaj13

There are three main types of 13th chord, as shown in the table below.

In practice, it is not possible to play all seven notes of a 13th chord on guitar, therefore some notes (normally the 9th, 11th and sometimes the 5th) are omitted.

There are several of different fingerings for the major 13th chord. Which one you use depends on which chord you want to play next, so your fingers are ready to move quickly.

Chord Spelling for 13ths	
13 (Dominant 13th):	1 3 5 ♭7 9 11 13
m13 (Minor 13th):	1 ♭3 5 ♭7 9 11 13
maj13 (Major 13th):	1 3 5 7 9 11 13

MORE CHORDS

START
HERE

ALL THE
BASICS

FIRST
CHORDS

TIMING
& CHARTS

NOTES
& KEYS

MORE
CHORDS

SCALES
& PITCH

MORE
SKILLS

C13

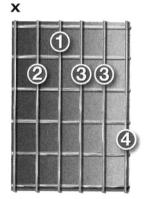

Cm13

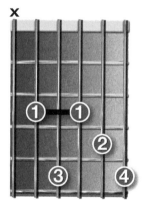

Cmaj13

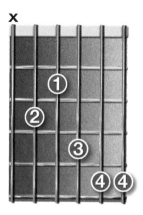

FREE ACCESS on iPhone & Android
etc, using any free QR code app

Scan to **HEAR** chords and scales, or
go directly to flametreemusic.com

Altered Chords

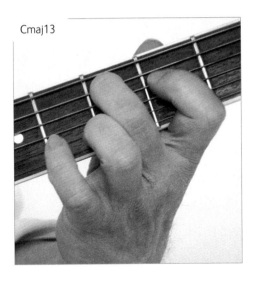

Cmaj13

These are chords in which the fifth and/or ninth has been 'altered' – i.e. either raised or lowered by a half step.

Altered chords are most commonly used in jazz. These are examples of the most commonly used.

START HERE

ALL THE BASICS

RHYTHM & NOTES

TIMING & CHARTS

NOTES & KEYS

MORE CHORDS

SCALES & PITCH

MORE SKILLS

Chord	Chord Spelling
Augmented triad:	1 3 ♯5
Diminished triad:	1 ♭3 ♭5
Diminished 7th:	1 ♭3 ♭5 ♭♭7
Dominant 7th ♭5:	1 3 ♭5 ♭7
Dominant 7th ♭9:	1 3 5 ♭7 ♭9
Dominant 7th ♯9:	1 3 5 ♭7 ♯9

Chord Substitution

You can make your own interpretations of chords in a songbook by using chord inversions, embellishments and substitutions instead of the original chords. You can also use this approach when songwriting, by starting with a simple chord progression and turning it into something quite elaborate.

Chord Embellishment

Chord embellishment consists of varying a chord by **substituting** a note within it for a new note, or by **adding** an extra note. Whichever method is used, the new note should be taken from the 'key scale' of the chord: for example, you could add any note from the C major scale to the C major chord without changing the fundamental harmonic nature of the chord.

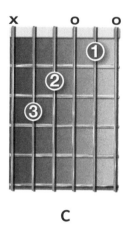

C

Cmaj11

By sticking to notes from the key scale, the new embellished chord can normally be used as a direct replacement for the simpler basic chord without causing any clashes with the melody of the song.

Chord embellishments are often easier to play than the basic major or minor chords.

If you lift the finger off the first string when playing an open position D major chord shape, it will become a Dsus2 chord.

D

Dsus2

Adding an extra note to a chord is also an effective way of creating an embellishment. The **ninth note** of the major scale is often used, as this creates a certain warmth when added to a basic major chord.

MORE CHORDS

In this example the ninth note (D) of the C major key is added to the C major chord.

C

Cmaj/9

The same approach can be taken with **minor** and **dominant** seventh chords.

The table below gives examples of the most commonly used chord embellishments – none of which will cause problems within an existing chord progression as the basic chord's harmonic nature will not be changed.

Basic Chord	Possible Embellishments
Major	major 6th, major 7th, major 9th, add 9, sus2, sus4, major 6th add 9
Minor	minor 7th, minor 9th, sus2, sus4
Dominant 7th	dominant 9th, dominant 13th, dominant 7th sus4

Chord Inversions

Rather than play every chord starting from its root note, you can play an 'inversion' by choosing another chord tone as the lowest note. There are three main types of inversion:

First inversion
Third of the chord is played as the lowest note.

Second inversion
Fifth of the chord is played as the lowest note.

Third inversion
Extension of the chord is played as the lowest note.

Inversions are normally notated as 'slash chords'

C/E is 'C major first inversion'

C/G is 'C major second inversion'

C/B is 'C major 7th third inversion'

MORE
CHORDS

C/E

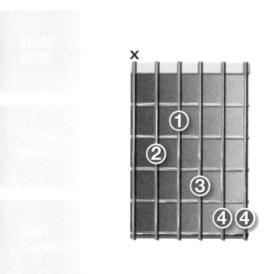

C/G

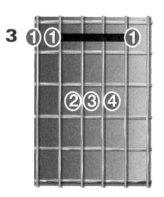

Cmaj7/B

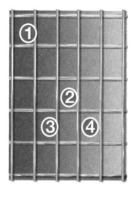

Full Chord Substitution

An interesting effect can be achieved by substituting one chord for another. For example, a major chord might be replaced by its 'relative minor' (i.e. the minor chord with a root note three half steps lower). For instance, **A minor** might be **substituted** for **C major**.

Alternatively, a minor chord could be replaced by its 'relative major' (i.e. the major chord with a root note three half steps higher). For example, **C major** might be substituted in place of **A minor**.

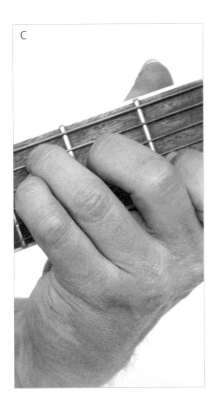

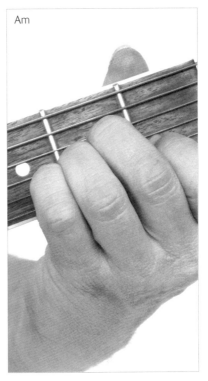

ABOVE: Simple substitution can create new directions for your sound.

MORE CHORDS

FREE ACCESS on iPhone & Android etc, using any free QR code app

Scan to **HEAR** chords and scales, or go directly to flametreemusic.com

Changing Chords

It's one thing to know some chord shapes, but it's a far more difficult skill to change fluently between them without leaving any gaps. Luckily, there are a few shortcuts you can take to make your chord changes easier and faster.

Minimum Movement Principle

It's essential that chord changes are crisp and prompt. This might not be too hard when using chords that you're very familiar with, but it can seem daunting with chords that are new to you. However, changing between any chords can be made much easier if you follow the 'minimum movement

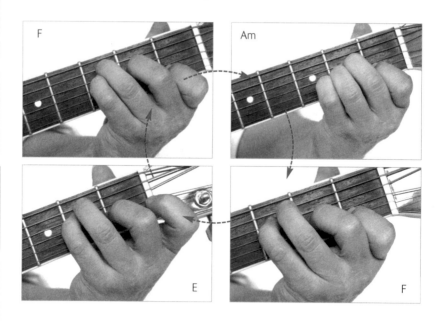

ABOVE: Finding the most economical fingering will increase your speed of change. Note here that E major is played using three of the same fingers as the F7, but one fret down.

principle'. This involves making only the smallest finger movement necessary between chords, and avoiding taking fingers off strings or frets only to put them back on again for the next chord.

Excess movement between chords is what slows chord changes down; **the less your fingers move, the faster your chord changes will be**.

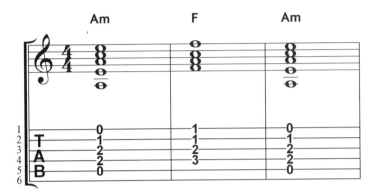

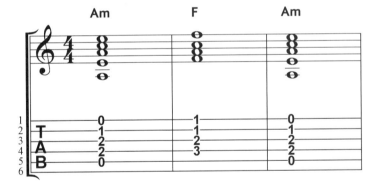

ABOVE and OVERLEAF: When moving from Am to F, keep the first finger on the second string first fret, but flatten it to cover the first string as well. Between Am and C only move the third finger; keep the others in place. Notice how E major is the same 'shape' as Am – just on different strings.

MORE
CHORDS

Some chords have one or more notes in common. For example, the open position A minor and F major chords **both include the note C** (first fret on the B string). The C major chord also includes this note and, in addition, has another note in common with the A minor chord (E on the second fret of the D string). The chord progression shown on the previous page uses the chords Am, F and E: notice the **common fingering** between each chord change; in particular, how the **first finger stays on the first fret** and how the **second finger stays on the second fret** throughout.

Even if different chords don't contain too many common notes, changing between them can still be made easier if you **look out for any possible links**. For example, when changing between the D and A major chords the **third finger can be slid along the second string** (between frets two and three) rather than being taken off the string only to be put back on a fret higher a moment later.

Following the principle of minimum movement saves time and makes the chord changes smoother. No matter how remote a chord change appears to be, there will always be some kind of link between the chords; once spotted, this will make changing between them easier.

MORE
CHORDS

ABOVE: Try to spot the common links between consecutive chord shapes. For example, between the D and A chords the third finger could just slide along the second string, while the first and second fingers move up or down across the strings.

Barre Chords

Playing open position chords is a great way to begin learning the guitar, but if you take a careful look at any professional players you'll soon notice that most of their chord positions are further up the fretboard; more often than not they'll be playing shapes known as 'barre chords'.

Advantages of Barre Chords

Playing a barre chord involves re-fingering an open position chord so as to leave the first finger free to play the barre by fretting all six strings. The whole chord can then be moved up the fingerboard to different pitches.

The main advantage of using barre chords is that you can move the same shape up or down the fingerboard to create new chords without the need to memorize a whole host of different fingerings for each chord. Using barre chords will allow you to play more unusual chords (like B♭ minor or F♯ major), which are unobtainable in open position.

MORE
CHORDS

ABOVE: Barre chords are useful because a single hand position can be used for all of the 12 different keys simply by moving it up or down the neck of the guitar.

FREE ACCESS on iPhone & Android
etc, using any free QR code app

Scan to **HEAR** chords and scales, or
go directly to flametreemusic.com

Major Barre Chords

To play major chords in barre form, begin by re-fingering an open position
E major chord using the second, third and fourth fingers. Then move this up to
different fingerboard positions, with the first finger fretting all the strings on
the adjacent lower fret. Most guitars have marker dots on frets three, five and
seven, and moving the barre of the **E major shape** to these positions will
give the chords of **G, A** and **B major**.

In theory, you could play all major chords with just this one barre chord shape.
In practice, however, this would involve leaping around the fingerboard too
much when changing from one chord to another. Therefore, knowing at least
two shapes for each chord type will enable you to play through most songs
without ever having to shift more than a couple of frets for each chord change.

The second major shape you can convert to a barre chord is the open position
A major shape; moving this shape with the barre on the marker dots on frets
three, five and seven of the A string will give the chords of C, D and E major.

MORE CHORDS

G major barre chord – based upon
an **E major shape**. Move this shape
to the fifth fret for A major and to the
seventh fret for B major.

C major barre chord – based upon
an **A major shape**. Move this shape
to the fifth fret for D major and the
seventh fret for E major.

Minor Barre Chords

Open position minor chords can also be converted to barre chords. The E minor and A minor shapes can be re-fingered to leave the first finger free to make the barre.

When the **E minor shape** is moved up, the pitch of the chord should be taken from the barre position on the E string.

When the **A minor chord** is moved up, the pitch should be taken from the barre position on the A string.

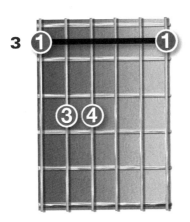

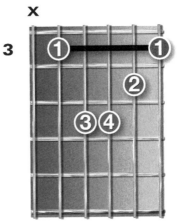

G minor barre chord – based upon an **E minor shape**. Move this shape to the fifth fret for A minor and to the seventh fret for B minor.

C minor barre chord – based upon an **A minor shape**. Move this shape to the fifth fret for D minor and to the seventh fret for E minor.

MORE
CHORDS

Mixing Barre Chords

Most songs will combine a mixture of major and minor chords. Whether you decide to use an E or A shape barre chord will depend on the position of the previous and the following chord; the trick is to choose the shape that will avoid any large fingerboard shifts.

FREE ACCESS on iPhone & Android etc, using any free QR code app

Scan to **HEAR** chords and scales, or go directly to flametreemusic.com

Major Scales

By far the most important scale in music is the major scale. All other scales, and even all chords, can be considered as stemming from the major scale.

The major scale is used as the basis for the majority of popular melodies. When used in lead playing it gives a bright and melodic sound.

Scale Construction

C	plus a **whole** step	=	**D**
D	plus a **whole** step	=	**E**
E	plus a **half** step	=	**F**
F	plus a **whole** step	=	**G**
G	plus a **whole** step	=	**A**
A	plus a **whole** step	=	**B**
B	plus a **half** step	=	**C**

FREE ACCESS on iPhone & Android etc, using any free QR code app

Scan to **HEAR** chords and scales, or go directly to flametreemusic.com

SCALES & PITCH

The **major scale** is constructed by using a combination of **whole** steps/whole tones (**W**) and **half** steps/semitones (**H**). Regardless of the key, the pattern of tones and semitones for the major key is as follows:

W W H W W W H

For example, the **C major scale** is constructed as follows:

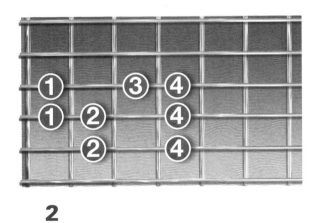

ABOVE: C major scale: notation, TAB and fingering.

Transposing Scales

All the scales illustrated in this chapter are 'transpositional': they can be played in other keys simply by **starting the finger pattern at a different fret**.

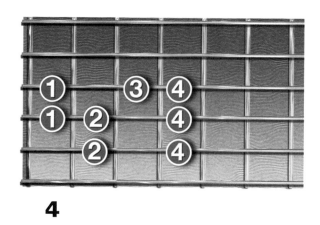

ABOVE: D major scale: notation, TAB and fingering.

For example, to play the **D major scale** (opposite), use the exact fingering shown for C major but **start two frets higher**.

For some keys, for example G major (below), you might prefer to start the scale pattern on the low E string in order to avoid high fingerboard positions.

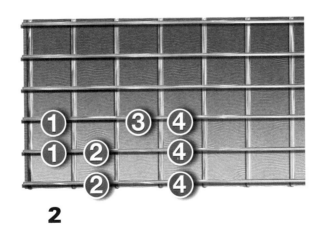

ABOVE: G major scale: notation, TAB and fingering.

START HERE

ALL THE BASICS

RHYTHM & NOTES

TIMING & CHARTS

NOTES & KEYS

MORE CHORDS

SCALES & PITCH

MORE SKILLS

Pentatonic Major Scale

The term 'pentatonic' means '**five-note**'; the pentatonic major scale is a
five-note abbreviation of the standard major scale, with the fourth and seventh
degrees of the major scale omitted. For example, the notes in the **C major
scale** are **C D E F G A B**. To convert this into the C pentatonic major scale
omit the notes F (the 4th) and B (the 7th), resulting in **C D E G A**.

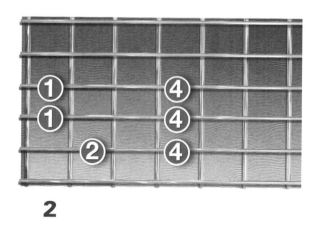

2

ABOVE: C pentatonic major scale: notation, TAB and fingering.

SCALES
& PITCH

The pentatonic major scale has none of the overtly sugary sound often associated with the standard major scale – instead it has a great combination of brightness with a cutting edge. It is a very useful scale for improvising in major keys; because it contains fewer notes than the standard major scale there is less chance of any of the notes clashing with the accompanying chords.

Traditionally, pentatonic major scales have been used in country music, but many rock bands – from the **Rolling Stones** (Keith Richards below) and **Free** to **Travis** and **Supergrass** – have used them frequently on their recordings. Brit-rock bands were great fans of the pentatonic major scale, particularly Noel Gallagher, who relied on them almost exclusively for his solos on the first few **Oasis** albums. Some of its greatest exponents are country-rock players like Albert Lee and Danny Gatton.

SCALES
& PITCH

FREE ACCESS on iPhone & Android etc, using any free QR code app

Scan to **HEAR** chords and scales, or go directly to flametreemusic.com

Minor Scales

There are a variety of minor scales to suit all musical styles, from the soulful natural minor scale to the exotic harmonic minor scale.

However, the rock-edged pentatonic minor scale is by far the most widely-used scale in lead-guitar playing.

Natural Minor Scale

C	plus a **whole** step	=	D
C	plus a **whole** step	=	D
D	plus a **half** step	=	E♭
E♭	plus a **whole** step	=	F
F	plus a **whole** step	=	G
G	plus a **half** step	=	A♭
A♭	plus a **whole** step	=	B♭
B♭	plus a **whole** step	=	C

START HERE

ALL THE BASICS

FIRST CHORDS

TIMING & CHARTS

NOTES & KEYS

MORE CHORDS

SCALES & PITCH

MORE SKILLS

FREE ACCESS on iPhone & Android etc, using any free QR code app

Scan to **HEAR** chords and scales, or go directly to flametreemusic.com

The **natural minor scale** is constructed using a particular combination of **whole** steps/tones (**W**) and **half** steps/semitones (**H**) in the following pattern:

W H W W H W W

For example, C natural minor scale is constructed as follows:

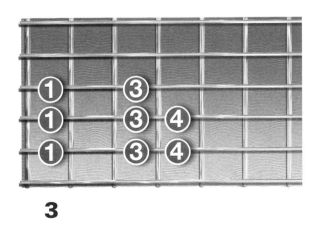

3

SCALES
& PITCH

ABOVE: C natural minor scale: notation, TAB and fingering.

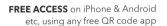

The interval spelling for the natural minor scale is 1 2 ♭3 4 5 ♭6 ♭7 8, meaning that, in comparison to the major scale with the same keynote, the third, sixth and seventh notes are flattened by a half step. The natural minor scale is widely used in rock- and blues-based music. The scale has a soulful, yet melodic sound. Carlos Santana and Samantha Fish (below) are two of its high-profile exponents.

Pentatonic Minor Scale

In all forms of rock music, the pentatonic minor scale is the most commonly-used scale for lead-guitar playing. The interval spelling is 1 ♭3 4 5 ♭7 8. It is a popular scale for improvising in minor keys because it contains fewer notes than the natural minor scale – this makes the scale easy to use and means that there is little chance of any of the notes clashing with the accompanying chords.

SCALES & PITCH

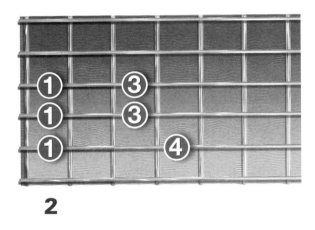

2

ABOVE: C pentatonic minor scale: notation, TAB and fingering.

Harmonic Minor Scale

The harmonic minor scale is very similar to the natural minor scale. The only difference is that, in the harmonic minor scale, the note on the seventh degree is raised by a half step. This results in a large interval between the sixth and seventh degrees of the scale, giving the scale its distinctive, exotic sound.

SCALES
& PITCH

FREE ACCESS on iPhone & Android etc, using any free QR code app

Scan to **HEAR** chords and scales, or go directly to flametreemusic.com

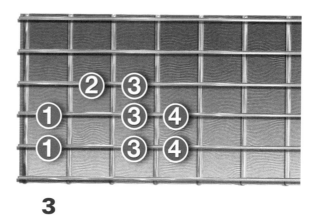

ABOVE: C harmonic minor scale: notation, TAB and fingering.

The interval spelling is 1 2 ♭3 4 5 ♭6 7 8. Ritchie Blackmore (Deep Purple and Rainbow) was one of the first rock guitarists to exploit the melodic potential of this scale.

SCALES
& PITCH

Scan to **HEAR** chords and scales, or go directly to flametreemusic.com

Melodic Minor Scale

The step pattern of this scale alters depending on whether it is being played **ascending** or **descending**. When played **descending** it has the same notes as the **natural minor scale**; when played ascending the sixth and seventh degrees are each raised by a half step. The interval spelling is 1 2 ♭3 4 5 6 7 8 ascending and 1 2 ♭3 4 5 ♭6 ♭7 8 descending. The scale is mostly used in jazz rock and fusion.

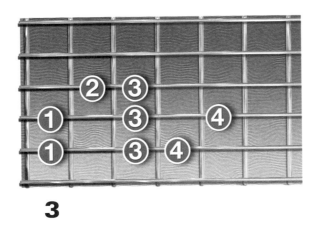

ABOVE: C melodic minor scale ascending: notation, TAB and fingering.

Scan to **HEAR** chords and scales, or go directly to flametreemusic.com

SCALES & PITCH

Pitch

In this section, scales have been shown with a starting note of C. You can alter the pitch of any scale easily by starting the same finger pattern at a different fret.

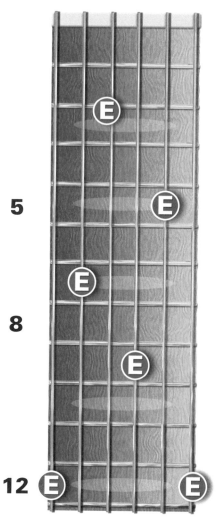

However, you may need to change the fingering for each scale to play it in a higher or lower octave – or simply in a different fingerboard position.

Fingerboard Positions

One of the interesting things about the guitar fingerboard is that the same note can be played at exactly the same pitch in several different places on the fingerboard.

If you play through the example on the right, you'll notice that each E note has a slightly different tonal quality even though they all have the same pitch.

SCALES & PITCH

The same applies to scales and riffs – they will have a slightly different tone depending upon the chosen fingerboard position.

You will also find that some riffs or licks might be easier to play in one fingerboard position compared to another.

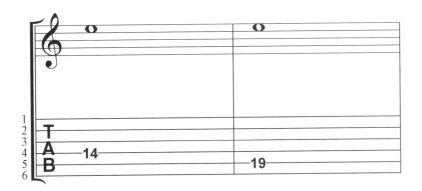

ABOVE: The note of E can be played at exactly the same pitch in six different fingerboard positions, three of which are shown LEFT.

FREE ACCESS on iPhone & Android etc, using any free QR code app

Scan to **HEAR** chords and scales, or go directly to flametreemusic.com

SCALES
& PITCH

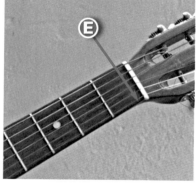

E on the open top E string

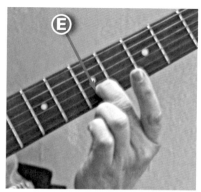

E on the fifth fret (B string)

E on the 9th fret (G string)

FREE ACCESS on iPhone & Android
etc, using any free QR code app

Scan to **HEAR** chords and scales, or
go directly to flametreemusic.com

SCALES
& PITCH

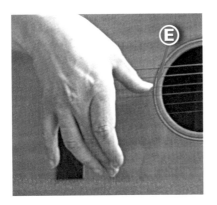

E: 14th fret (D string)

E: 19th fret (A string)

If you're really serious about studying the guitar, you should make it a long-term aim to learn as many different fingerboard positions as possible for all your scales, because this will provide you with the maximum amount of flexibility in your playing.

To start you on your way, over the page are **three positions** of the **C major scale** – all at the same pitch.

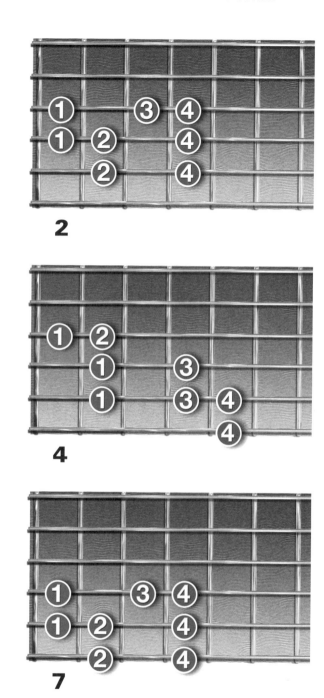

2

4

7

START HERE

ALL THE BASICS

FIRST CHORDS

TIMING & CHARTS

NOTES & KEYS

MORE CHORDS

SCALES & PITCH

MORE SKILLS

FREE ACCESS on iPhone & Android etc, using any free QR code app

Scan to **HEAR** chords and scales, or go directly to flametreemusic.com

Changing Octave: Practising in C Major

As well as learning scales of the same pitch in different fingerboard positions, you also need to be able to play them in different octaves. This will give you a wider sonic range to play across.

Greater fingerboard knowledge will help you play sympathetically with other elements in a song, for example, playing in a range that will merge well with the vocals or other instruments in some sections of the song, while moving to an octave that will make the guitar jump out of the mix in other sections.

Practising scales in a variety of fingerboard positions and **octaves** will help you develop a good knowledge of the location of notes on the fingerboard; this in turn will enable you to target notes that match the chord structure when improvising. Ideally, you should aim to develop a practice regime that will enable you, over a period of time, to **learn all the scales** in this book **in all keys** and in all possible **octaves** and **fingerboard positions**.

As a starting point, the fretboard diagrams on the next page show the same C major scale illustrated on page **131**. The scale is repeated on page **146**, then one and two octaves higher. Overleaf there are several different fingerboard positions showing the same scale on different srings.

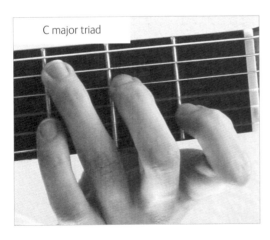

C major triad

Of course, all these scales can be played over the top of a simple C major triad. One guitar can play a rhythm with the chord, the other can play the scales. Then swap over.

START
HERE

ALL THE
BASICS

FIRST
CHORDS

TIMING
& CHARTS

NOTES
& KEYS

MORE
CHORDS

SCALES
& PITCH

MORE
SKILLS

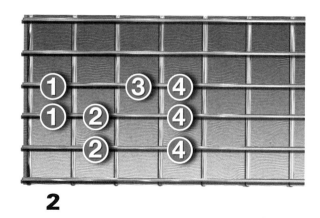

2

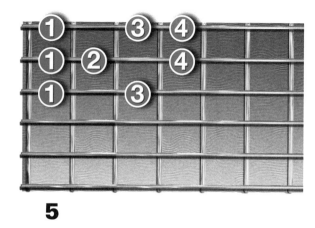

5

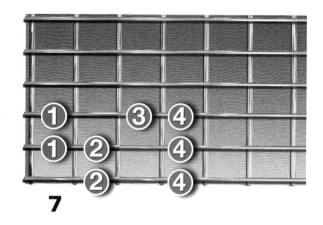

7

FREE ACCESS on iPhone & Android
etc, using any free QR code app

Scan to **HEAR** chords and scales, or
go directly to flametreemusic.com

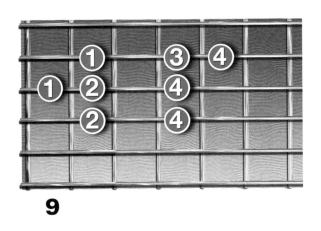

9

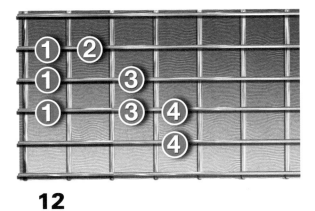

12

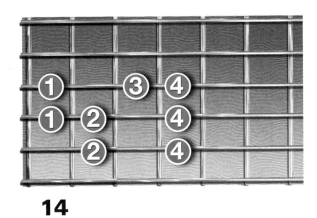

14

START
HERE

ALL THE
BASICS

RHYTHM
& NOTES

TIMING
& CHARTS

NOTES
& KEYS

MORE
CHORDS

SCALES
& PITCH

MORE
SKILLS

FREE ACCESS on iPhone & Android
etc, using any free QR code app

Scan to **HEAR** chords and scales, or
go directly to flametreemusic.com

Plectrum Technique

Most electric guitarists want to play fast, and developing great speed starts with having proper control over your plectrum. If you start by holding the plectrum the wrong way you can develop habits that will make it hard to become a fast and accurate player.

Gripping the Plectrum

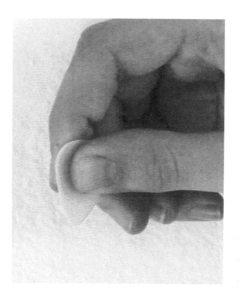

The best method is to grip the plectrum between the thumb and index finger. Position the plectrum so that its point is about half a centimetre ($\frac{1}{4}$ of an inch) beyond the fingertip. Use only the tip of the plectrum to pick the strings or you will create a physical resistance that will slow down your playing. However, bear in mind that if you show too little plectrum you might end up missing the string altogether.

Experiment until you get just the right balance. Also, be mindful of how you grip the plectrum. If you use too much pressure your hand muscles will tighten and so reduce your fluency, but if you hold it too loosely you'll keep dropping it.

Hold the plectrum so that it's in line with your fingernail. Avoid holding it at right angles to your index finger, as this will cause your wrist to lock.

Alternate Picking

If you want to achieve any degree of speed with the plectrum for lead playing then it's best to use 'alternate picking' as the mainstay of your plectrum technique. This involves alternating downstrokes and upstrokes. Alternate picking is the most logical and economical way of playing, since once you have picked a string downwards, the plectrum will then be ideally positioned to pick upwards, whereas if you try to play two downstrokes in a row you will need to raise the plectrum back up before you can strike the string again.

When alternating down- and upstrokes, make sure that the picking action is generated by swivelling the wrist; try to avoid moving the elbow up and down as this will make your picking style much too cumbersome and will hamper your fluency. For fast lead playing, alternate picking and a relaxed wrist action are the fundamental requirements.

Picking Exercises

Begin by practising alternate picking on the open sixth string. Once you have a secure plectrum technique you can make your licks sound faster by doubling, or even quadrupling, your picking on some notes, on each string.

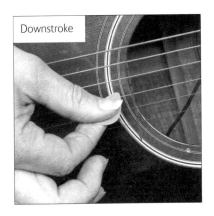
Downstroke

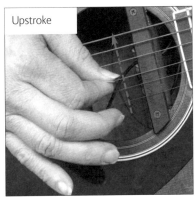
Upstroke

MORE SKILLS

The fretting hand may be moving quite slowly, but the lick will sound more mobile because of the activity of the picking hand. Practise this technique at first by playing scales with double and quadruple picking.

A fast rock sound can be achieved by mixing fretted notes with an open string – while the right hand keeps picking with alternate down- and upstrokes.

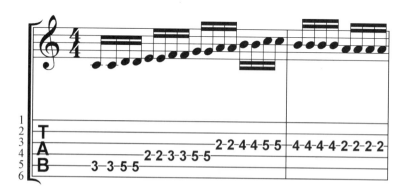

ABOVE: C major scale, played ascending with double picking, descending with quadruple picking.

Triplet Picking

A great way of making your playing sound super-fast is to use triplet picking patterns. Because these patterns cut across the standard $\frac{4}{4}$ rhythm, they give the impression of being much faster than they really are. This repeated 'down-up-down' picking style can give a rolling or galloping effect to a piece of music. (The term 'triplet' here refers only to the three-part picking action; the rhythm doesn't have to be a triplet in the traditional musical sense.)

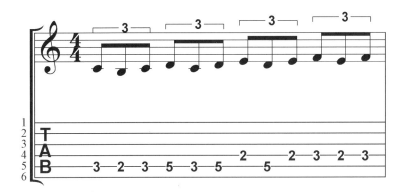

ABOVE: Use a 'down-up-down' picking pattern for each triplet.

Alternative Tunings

Discover a new range of beautiful chordal harmonies by simply tuning your guitar in a different way. If you sometimes start to feel restricted by sticking to the same chord shapes you've played before, then experimenting with alternative tunings is a great way of generating some fresh sounds and ideas.

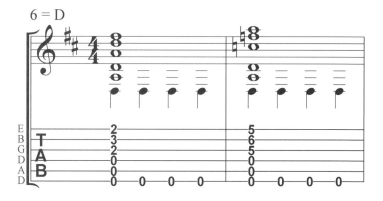

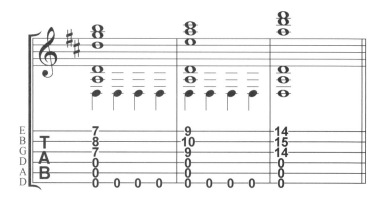

ABOVE: Dropped D tuning.

FREE ACCESS on iPhone & Android etc, using any free QR code app

Scan to **HEAR** chords and scales, or go directly to flametreemusic.com

Dropped D Tuning

There are numerous ways in which a guitar can be retuned, but the simplest and most common is 'dropped D tuning'. All you need to do is **lower** the **pitch** of the low **E string** by a **whole step** until it reaches the note of D (an octave lower than the open fourth string). You can check that you've retuned correctly by playing on the seventh fret of the sixth string and comparing the note to the open fifth string – they should produce exactly the same pitch.

Dropped D tuning is perfect for playing songs in the keys of D major or D minor. Having the low D bass string is almost like having your own built-in bass player – it can add great solidity and power to your sound. To make the most of this bass effect many guitarists use the low D string as a 'drone' – i.e. they repeatedly play this low D note while moving chord shapes up and down the fingerboard. Moving a simple D major shape up the fingerboard while playing a low D drone produces a very effective sound.

D Modal Tuning

Tuning the sixth, second and first strings down a whole step creates what is known as 'D modal tuning': **D A D G A D**. When you need to reach this tuning unaided just remember that the **A, D and G strings** are **tuned** as **normal**. Playing the open D string will give you the pitch for the lowered sixth string when it is played at the 12th fret. Playing the A string at the 12th fret will give you the pitch to tune the second string down to, and playing the D string at the 12th fret will give you the pitch to tune the first string down to.

Once the guitar is correctly tuned it will give you a **Dsus4 chord** when the open strings are all strummed, thus creating instant ambiguity and a sense of interest. When first using this tuning, playing in the key of D will prove the easiest: by placing the first finger on the second fret of the G string you will make a nice deep-sounding D major (D5) chord.

Traditional chord shapes will not work in the same way with any altered tuning, so it's really a case of experimenting to find chord sounds that you like. The secret is to be adventurous and see what ideas you can come up with when freed from the restrictions of conventional chord shapes.

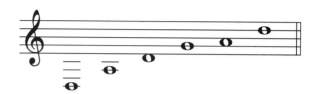

ABOVE: D modal tuning.

Other Tunings

If the two altered tunings described above have given you the taste for experimentation, then here are a few other tunings you can try (all shown starting with the low sixth string).

Slack key tuning – D G D G B D (the first, fifth and sixth strings are 'slackened' down a whole step to form a G major chord).

Open E tuning – E B E G♯ B E (the third, fourth and fifth strings are tuned higher than normal to make an E major chord).

Open D tuning – D A D F♯ A D (the first, second, third and sixth strings are tuned down so that the open strings form a D major chord).

ABOVE: Slack key tuning.

ABOVE: Open E tuning.

ABOVE: Open D tuning.

FREE ACCESS on iPhone & Android etc, using any free QR code app

Scan to **HEAR** chords and scales, or go directly to flametreemusic.com

MORE SKILLS

Basic Arpeggios

Learning arpeggios is a good way of developing a comprehensive knowledge of the guitar fingerboard. But arpeggios aren't just technical exercises – they're great for soloing and can make your lead playing more melodic by emphasizing the harmonic structure of the underlying chord progression.

Constructing Arpeggios

An arpeggio is simply the **notes** of a **chord** played **individually**. Standard major and minor chords, and therefore their arpeggios, contain only three different notes. For example, if you look closely at the open position C major chord you'll notice that although you're playing five strings, there are in fact only three different notes (**C E G**) in the chord. If you play these notes consecutively, rather than strum them simultaneously, then you've created a **C major arpeggio**.

When you're first learning arpeggios it's helpful to practise them in the set order (i.e. **1st**, **3rd**, **5th**, **8th**), but once you know them you can improvise freely by swapping the notes around, or repeating some, to make up an interesting lick or riff, just as you would when improvising with a scale.

C major

The really useful thing is that, because the **C major arpeggio** contains exactly the same notes as the **C major chord**, whatever notes you play from the C major arpeggio when improvising will always be totally in tune with a C major chord accompaniment.

Scan to **HEAR** chords and scales, or go directly to flametreemusic.com

ABOVE: C major arpeggio.

BELOW: Playing a C major arpeggio.

A string, C bass note

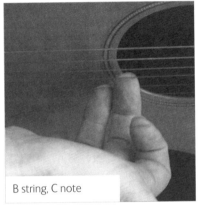

B string, C note

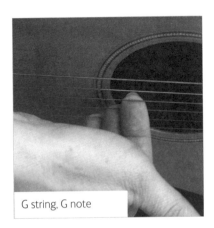

G string, G note

E string, E note

MORE SKILLS

FREE ACCESS on iPhone & Android etc, using any free QR code app

Scan to **HEAR** chords and scales, or go directly to flametreemusic.com

Major and Minor Arpeggios

Each basic major or minor arpeggio will only contain three notes; you can work out which notes these are by analyzing the relevant chord shape. A major arpeggio always contains the first, third and fifth notes of the major scale with the same starting note (for example, C E G are the 1st, 3rd and 5th notes of the C major scale and so form the C major arpeggio).

To work out minor arpeggios flatten the third note of the major arpeggio by a half step (e.g. C minor arpeggio contains the notes C E♭ G).

Aim to acquire knowledge of all major and minor arpeggios in as many finger-board positions as possible. Here are some fingerboard positions for C major and C minor arpeggios. They can be transposed to other pitches by moving them up or down the fingerboard.

Using Arpeggios

You can use arpeggios for riffs and lead playing. When you use a scale for a lead solo you'll notice that some notes sound more resolved against certain chords than other notes. This problem disappears when you use arpeggios; the notes of each arpeggio are taken from the chords they will all sound completely 'in tune' – providing you're playing the right arpeggio for each chord.

If you've only used scales before, this takes a little getting used to as you'll need to change arpeggio every time there is a chord change.

In a normal playing situation guitarists rarely use arpeggios throughout a whole solo, as this approach can tend to sound almost too 'in tune'. Instead, arpeggios are used to add colour over just a couple of chords, and the normal key scale is used for the majority of the solo.

MORE SKILLS

First C Major Arpeggio Pattern

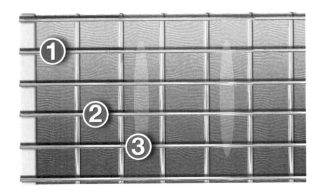

FREE ACCESS on iPhone & Android etc, using any free QR code app

Scan to **HEAR** chords and scales, or go directly to flametreemusic.com

Second C Major Arpeggio Pattern

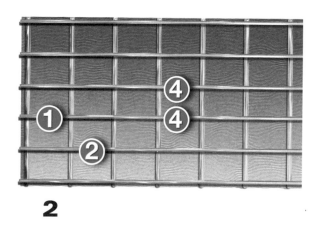

2

Third C Major Arpeggio Pattern

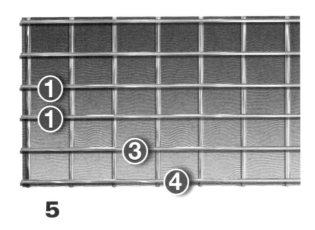

5

FREE ACCESS on iPhone & Android
etc, using any free QR code app

Scan to **HEAR** chords and scales, or
go directly to flametreemusic.com

First C Minor Arpeggio Pattern

START
HERE

ALL THE
BASICS

FIRST
CHORDS

TIMING
& CHARTS

NOTES
& KEYS

MORE
CHORDS

SCALES
& PITCH

MORE
SKILLS

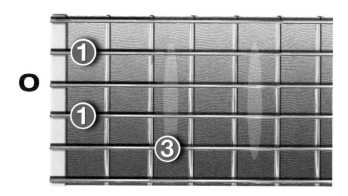

FREE ACCESS on iPhone & Android
etc, using any free QR code app

Scan to **HEAR** chords and scales, or
go directly to flametreemusic.com

Second C Minor Arpeggio Pattern

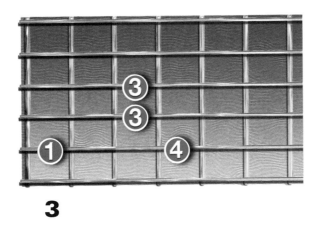

3

Third C Minor Arpeggio Pattern

START
HERE

ALL THE
BASICS

FIRST
CHORDS

TIMING
& CHARTS

NOTES
& KEYS

MORE
CHORDS

SCALES
& PITCH

MORE
SKILLS

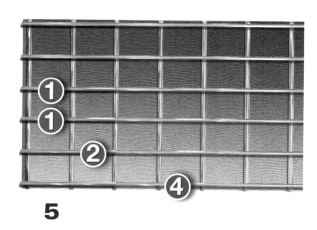

5

More Arpeggios

Once you've learnt the basic major and minor arpeggios it's not too difficult to extend these to learn the arpeggios for other chords, such as sevenths and even extended and altered chords. A secure knowledge of arpeggios will mean that you'll always be able to improvise over any chord progression.

Seventh Arpeggios

These are formed by taking the notes of the relevant seventh chord and playing them in a scale-like pattern. There are three main types of seventh chord arpeggios: dominant seventh, minor seventh and major seventh. Although they have some notes in common, the sound varies considerably between each one: dominant sevenths are great for blues and R&B, minor sevenths are used a lot in both rock and funk, and major sevenths give a very melodic sound suited to ballads.

ABOVE: Hand position for C major 7th arpeggio (C E G B).

FREE ACCESS on iPhone & Android etc, using any free QR code app

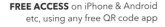

Scan to **HEAR** chords and scales, or go directly to flametreemusic.com

MORE
SKILLS

3   C dominant 7th arpeggio (C E G B♭).

2   C major 7th arpeggio (C E G B♭).

3   C minor 7th arpeggio (C E♭, G B♭).

Sixth Arpeggios

Major and minor sixth arpeggios are commonly used for creating riffs. The typical rock'n'roll riff below is taken directly from the C major sixth arpeggio.

Altered Arpeggios

One of the most useful applications of arpeggios is over altered chords, such as diminished or augmented chords. Although you may have difficulty choosing a scale to improvise over such chords, arpeggios will always work – because they contain exactly the same notes as the chords you cannot fail to play in tune. Therefore, a thorough knowledge of altered arpeggios will prove highly useful if you wish to improvise over advanced chord progressions, such as those used in jazz and fusion.

Overleaf are some of the most useful altered arpeggios. They are all illustrated with a root note of C, but can be easily transposed simply by starting at a different fingerboard position.

MORE SKILLS

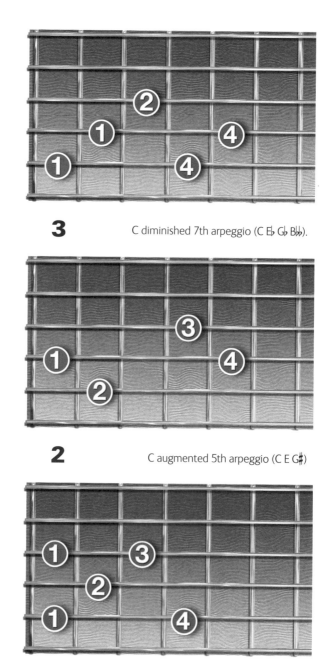

3 C diminished 7th arpeggio (C E♭ G♭ B♭♭).

2 C augmented 5th arpeggio (C E G♯)

3 C minor 7th ♭5 arpeggio (C E♭ G♭ B♭)

Scan to **HEAR** chords and scales, or
go directly to flametreemusic.com

**MORE
SKILLS**

Octaves

Octave playing is an instant way of giving more power and solidity to your playing, and because of this it is a technique that is often used by jazz and rock musicians alike. Learning octaves is also one of the quickest ways of getting to know all the notes on the fretboard.

Playing octaves involves playing two of the same notes together (e.g. C and C), but with one of those notes at a higher pitch (i.e. an octave above). The fact that the two notes are the same is what gives octave playing its powerful sound and avoids the excessive sweetness that is often associated with other pairings of notes.

Bass Octaves

There are various ways in which octaves can be played, but for notes on the bass strings by far the most common way is to add a note two frets and two strings higher. For example, if your original note is A on the fifth fret of the sixth string, then the octave A will be on the seventh fret of the fourth string.

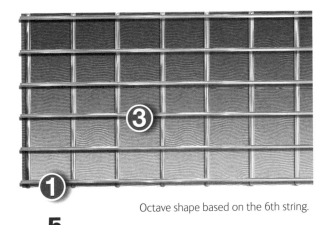

Octave shape based on the 6th string.

5

MORE SKILLS

Similarly, if your original note is D on the fifth fret of the fifth string, then the octave D will be on the seventh fret of the third string.

This system of finding the octave two frets and two strings higher than the original note will work for all notes on the sixth and fifth strings. The lower note should be played with the first finger, while the octave can be fretted with either the third or the fourth finger.

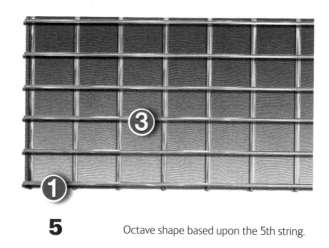

5   Octave shape based upon the 5th string.

The most important technique when playing bass octaves is to ensure that the string between the lower note and the octave is totally muted. This should be done by allowing the first finger to lie across it lightly – not fretting the string but just deadening it.

You should also be careful not to strum the strings above the octave note, and as a precaution it's a good idea to mute them by allowing the octave-fretting finger to lightly lie across them.

RIGHT: A bass octave slide can be achieved by moving your hand up or down two frets along one string.

MORE
SKILLS

Treble Octaves

The easiest way of playing octaves on the treble strings is to use a similar approach to that described above, but with the octave note requiring a further one-fret stretch. For the fourth and third strings the octave notes can be found by playing three frets and two strings higher. For example, if your original note is G on the fifth fret of the fourth string then the octave G will be on the eighth fret of the second string. This system of finding the octave three frets and two strings higher than the original note will work for all notes on the fourth and third strings.

MORE SKILLS

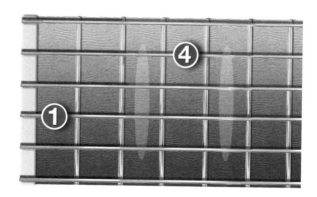

Octave shape based upon the 4th string.

Octave shape based upon the 3rd string.

START
HERE

ALL THE
BASICS

FIRST
CHORDS

TIMING
& CHARTS

NOTES
& KEYS

MORE
CHORDS

SCALES
& PITCH

MORE
SKILLS

Playing Octaves

Once you're familiar with the octave shapes shown above, try to play through the examples of octave use given below.

ABOVE: Sixth string octave riff. Notice how much stronger this riff sounds when it is played the second time with the octave note added.

ABOVE: Sixth and fifth string octaves. Using octaves starting from two strings can minimize the amount of fingerboard movement needed. Just be careful to strum the correct strings and make sure that unwanted strings between the fretted notes are fully muted.

MORE SKILLS

flametreemusic.com

The Flame Tree Music website complements our range of print books and offers easy access to chords and scales online, and on the move, through tablets, smartphones, and desktop computers.

1. The site offers access to chord diagrams and finger positions for both the guitar and the piano/keyboard, presenting a wide range of sound options to help develop good listening technique, and to assist you in identifying the chord and each note within it.

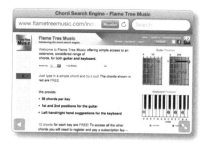

2. The site offers 12 **free** chords, those most commonly used in bands and songwriting.

3. A subscription is available if you'd like the full range of chords, **50** for **each key**.

4. Guitar chords are shown with **first** and **second positions on the fretboard**.

5. For the keyboard, you can **see** and **hear** each note in **left-** and **right-hand positions**.

6. Choose the key, then the chord name from the drop down menu. Note that the **red chords** are available **free**. Those in blue can be accessed with a subscription.

7. Once you've selected the chord, press **GO** and the details of the chord will be shown, with chord spellings, keyboard and guitar fingerings.

8. Sounds are provided in four easy-to-understand configurations.

9. flametreemusic.com also gives you access to **20 scales for each key**.